DON'T SUFFER, COMMUNICATE!

A ZEN GUIDE TO COMPASSIONATE COMMUNICATION

CHERI HUBER
ASHWINI NARAYANAN

DESIGNED & ILLUSTRATED BY JUNE SHIVER

Cover design by Marie Denkinger
sunwheelart@earthlink.net

Illustrated by
June Shiver
Ashwini Narayanan
Cheri Huber

Books by Cheri Huber and Ashwini Narayanan

Published by Keep It Simple Books

The Big Bamboozle: How You Get Conned Out of the Life You Want and What to Do about It

What Universe Are You Creating? Zen and the Art of Recording and Listening

I Don't Want To, I Don't Feel Like It: How Resistance Controls Your Life and What to Do about It

Books by Cheri Huber

What You Practice Is What You Have: A Guide to Having the Life You Want

There Is Nothing Wrong With You: Going Beyond Self-Hate, Rev. Ed.

The Fear Book: Facing Fear Once and for All, Rev. Ed.

The Depression Book: Depression as an Opportunity for Spiritual Growth, Expanded and Revised

Transform Your Life: A Year of Awareness Practice

The Key and the Name of the Key Is Willingness

Be the Person You Want to Find: Relationship and Self-Discovery

How You Do Anything Is How You Do Everything, Rev. Ed.

Suffering Is Optional: Three Keys to Freedom and Joy

When You're Falling, Dive: Acceptance, Possibility and Freedom

That Which You Are Seeking Is Causing You to Seek

There Is Nothing Wrong With You for Teens

Nothing Happens Next: Responses to Questions about Meditation

Time-Out for Parents: A Guide to Compassionate Parenting, Rev. Ed.

Trying to Be Human: Zen Talks

Sweet Zen: Dharma Talks with Cheri Huber

Good Life: Zen Precepts Retreat with Cheri Huber

The Zen Monastery Cookbook: Stories and Recipes from a Zen Kitchen

There Are No Secrets: Zen Meditation with Cheri Huber (DVD)

How to Get from Where You Are to Where You Want to Be
Published by Hay House

Unconditional Self-Acceptance: A Do-It-Yourself Course (6 CD set)
Published by Sounds True

Dedication

Compassionate Speech that Makes for Clarity
-- from *the Daily Recollection*

Acknowledgments

Thank you to the participants of the email class on communication who contributed the rich material for this book. We hope you'll forgive us for having taken the liberty of modifying your submissions.

Table of Contents

Practicing Compassionate Communication 179

In Gasshō 305

Really?
Another book on communication?

"We've just got to write that communication book." At least once a day I hear myself say this in response to the latest evidence of misery caused by poor or absent communication.

When I find myself saying, through gritted teeth, "I wish people would communicate," I usually mean that I wish people would stop listening to the voices in their head and get present enough to notice what is so *and say something.*

Here's an example: You notice a problem at work. The Internet is slow. The coffee machine is malfunctioning. A light bulb needs to be replaced. And you find yourself not saying something. Perhaps you think one or more of the following:

-- I don't want to be a bother.
-- I'm not going to be the bearer of bad news.
-- It's not my problem to fix.
-- Best not to get involved.
-- Perhaps it's just me.
-- It's not that bad.
-- Someone has probably reported it.

-- If no one else noticed, perhaps I shouldn't say anything.
-- Maybe they'll think I did it.
-- What if I'm asked to fix it!

The problem could be addressed if someone said something. So much suffering is caused because we listen to a voice in the head citing a thousand reasons not to say anything.

-- You can't say your partner hurt your feelings.
-- You can't say you would rather stay in than go out with friends.
-- You can't say you're interested in the new job posting because your boss would get upset.
-- You can't tell that expert investing your money that he's not doing a good job.
-- You can't ask for what you want.

Since it's been my life's work to attempt to assist people to end suffering, it's past time to tackle the misery that happens when people can't, won't, or choose not to communicate.

Dear Cheri,
     Wishing I had said something and
feeling bad that I did not is a place I
know well, along with saying something I wish I
hadn't! But this is what intrigues me. You
indicated that I'm listening to a voice in my head
telling me both not to say something and
prodding me to speak up. You make it sound like
something is controlling what comes out of my
mouth! Really?
Sincerely,
Disbelieving

Dear Disbelieving,
     Whether we believe it or not, something
usually IS controlling what we say and don't say.
We call what's interfering with our
communication egocentric karmic
conditioning/self-hate, ego for short.

We're usually not paying very close attention and we're not aware of ego taking over our attempts to communicate. It acts like a giant scrambler, distorting the signal, interpreting the information we receive, and scrambling what we transmit in response.

If we examine why we want to communicate well, we see that it's because we want to be seen, heard, and understood. We're looking for connection, validation, and acceptance. When we leave an interaction feeling dissatisfied, it's often because ego interfered with making the connection we were looking for. Identification with ego (explained below) leaves us feeling disconnected, from ourselves and from each other. Identification with ego maintains the disconnection, which is the opposite of what good communication achieves.

Perhaps a few examples might help. See if this sounds familiar...

Garbled Reception

Interrupted Transmission

Corrupted Reaction

Muddled Response

What we seek is connection. Identification with ego results in separation and isolation.
Gasshō,
ch

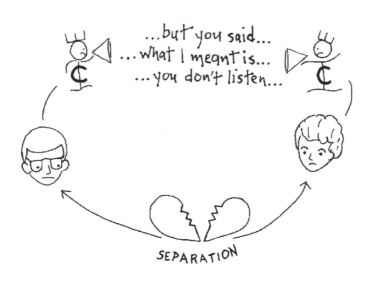

SEPARATION

Dear Cheri,
So, we're examining communication from the perspective of leaving egos out of it?
Sincerely,
Wanting to Clarify

Dear Wanting to Clarify,

That's correct. This book explores how identification with ego stops us from communicating and perpetuates suffering. The suffering is caused by **what is said** from identification with ego and by **what is not said** because of identification with ego. If egos were not (mis)communicating with each other, there would be far less suffering in the world!

Everything in this book is aimed at revealing egocentric karmic conditioning/self-hate in action. We explore how to bring conscious awareness to what we say, how we say it, what we believe about what we can and cannot say, what we're told before and after what we do and do not say. Awareness allows us to disidentify from ego, to step back into a wider perspective and be present in the moment in which we're living, and makes authentic communication possible.

Gasshō,

ch

Dear Cheri,
Egocentric karmic conditioning/self-hate sounds like a disease. Can you explain how I contracted it and how and why it affects communication?
Respectfully,
Wanting to Know

Dear Wanting to Know,
    Before explaining, we want to thank readers who are already familiar with our work for their patience as we cover what must seem like old territory once again. (For old-timers this would be an opportunity to take to heart the wisdom of Shunryu Suzuki, "If you lose the spirit of repetition, your practice will become quite difficult.")
    Around age 5-6, many of us gave up looking to our own experience and agreed, albeit unconsciously, that we'd be better off going along with what the people in charge of our survival were putting forth. We needed to survive. To survive we needed to please, in some degree, those people who held our survival in their hands. Would they have killed us

10

if we didn't go along? Probably not, but we didn't know that. At any rate, we began to look "outward" for direction. Regardless of our internal experience, we did comply. We began to accept the beliefs, opinions, philosophies, judgments, and attitudes of the people around us. When we hit the teenage years many of our number rebelled which simply consisted of adopting the opposite attitudes of the adults.

Being formed slowly throughout that process was one or more identities—collectively referenced as ego.

TIMELINE
I'm scared!
Cute is important.

I shouldn't do that!
I should be quiet.

I shouldn't be silly.
I am not good.

ME

We talk about ego as "the illusion of a self that is separate from Life." I am me. I am separate from, other than, everyone and everything else. Am I? Of course not, but it *feels* that way.

That feeling of being a separate self is created and maintained by an incessant "conversation" playing inside the head. We're conditioned to assume that the "conversation" is "me thinking."

IDENTIFICATION with ego is assuming the conversation is me thinking.

The conversation goes around the clock, "talking" about "me and my life." It tells me how to be, what to do, how to feel, what to think, what's right, wrong, good, bad, important, beautiful, ugly, valuable, along with one side or the other of every duality known to humanity. It reminds me of mistakes from the past, warns about mistakes in the future, worries, tells scary stories, threatens disasters, plans exciting adventures, fantasizes, procrastinates, wheedles, complains, judges, criticizes. It also talks to "me" about everyone else and what they're thinking, feeling, doing.

As we disidentify and observe our communication—or lack thereof—it becomes clear that most of the time the only communication we're engaged in is a back-and-forth between two or more voices/perspectives in the head. We call the participants in that conversation "the voices of ego."

A new neighbor invites me over for dinner...

Why do we call these ego voices? The voices are expressing the conditioned beliefs and assumptions that create and maintain an illusion that there's a real "I" that's other than, separate from, the rest of Life. We use the phrase egocentric karmic conditioning/self-hate to describe the various "expressions" of the illusion of a self that is separate from Life.

We can see in the example the conflict between ego perspectives that holds the illusion of "I" in place: I don't want to. I should want to. I'm a bad person for not wanting to. How I am is the cause of my life not working.

When we see that "just me thinking" is ego talking to ego, we will see conversation with other people in a new light.

Gasshō,

ch

Dear Cheri,
How does knowing about these voices in conditioned mind assist me to be a better communicator?

Sincerely,
Very Curious Now

Dear Very Curious Now,
I want to ask you to do an exercise before I answer that question.

Exercise ✏️

Look to see if right/wrong is an issue for you. Do you need to be the right person, fear being the wrong person, get told people think you're the wrong person, fear making a mistake, believe you'll be punished if you "do it wrong"?

Is good/bad an issue for you? Do you try to be a good person, fear you're bad, get told you're not a good person because of "sins and crimes" you commit, know who is good and who is bad, have a list of good qualities and bad qualities you could easily write down?

Does your world tend to fall out along "good/right person" and "bad/wrong person" duality lines?

✏️ **End of Exercise**

Did you do the exercise, Very Curious Now? If so, what did you notice? Were you surprised by how much your beliefs and opinions about right and wrong and good and bad influence your life? Did you notice how all of it happens in a conversation in your head?

Job #1 is becoming aware of the conversation in the head that keeps unconscious, unexamined beliefs and assumptions in place. Not being aware of unconscious, unexamined beliefs and assumptions keeps us trapped in the inability to communicate. We're too afraid of making a mistake, of doing it wrong, of being a bad person to risk saying something.

Once we're familiar with that conversation we can get on with the exciting exploration of communication. And catching on to that internal conversation is not as difficult as the internal conversation would like us to believe.

When we catch on to
the difference between believing
what's going on in the head and
the awareness that can observe
what's going on in the head,
we're inspired to let go the old
and practice the new.

For example, let's say I believe that I've always been too judgmental and feel like a failure because I haven't been able to stop judging. When I begin paying attention, I soon realize that "too judgmental" is a voice in my head. I realize it's no longer possible to say out loud to other people the things the voice says in my head, but the thoughts are still there. Now the judgmental voice is giving me grief, calling me a hypocrite for having the thoughts in my head and "pretending" I don't.

In Awareness Practice, there's no pretending. When we can see that "those thoughts/voices are not me, I'm not initiating them, I don't want them there, but there's nothing I can do to stop them," we don't need to fall for the hypocrite story. A quick way to check that out is to ask, "Do I want to have those judgments in my head, or would I choose not to have them if I could?" If you realize you don't want them and would get rid of them if you could, **you no longer have to take them personally or believe they're your responsibility!**

Realizing what egocentric karmic conditioning/self-hate is—a parasite, like mistletoe—assists us to step back, to stop believing its stories, and to practice redirecting the attention and choosing presence.

From presence, you don't have to do what the voices tell you to do, including their insistence that you should feel "bad." You don't have to say what the voices say. You don't have to give voice to the voices at all.

Gasshō,

ch

Dear Cheri,

Are you really saying that the voices in my head, that talk for me and control how I communicate, are not me? That I don't need to take responsibility for what comes out of my mouth?

Sincerely,

Responsible

Dear Responsible,

As you continue to watch, awareness will grow and sharpen. You'll have a sense of being "talked to." You'll see that what you experience as "you" is *listening* to that talk. You'll realize you're observing, watching, and hearing a back-and-forth in your head that you're not "doing."

You will realize that
you are not the voices in your head;
you are the awareness
that is aware of them.

For instance, you're getting ready for an activity, and because you're paying attention you become aware of a back-and-forth in conditioned mind (in your head): "You'd better call them to let them know you're going to be late," followed by, "I don't want to."

If you watch for a while, it's unmistakable that "you" are not initiating any of it. You're witnessing it. We are DEEPLY conditioned to believe "I'm thinking/doing/saying that," but careful observation makes it clear that, in fact, you're not.

 If you meditate, this quickly becomes obvious as you try to stop the yammering voices in conditioned mind and realize you can't. It's on its own program! That program, the one we call egocentric karmic conditioning/self-hate, flies under the radar. As soon as something goes awry—you say the wrong thing, you can't do something, you don't keep a commitment (any of a million things)—the voices pounce. In our example: "See, you knew you should have let them know! Now they're upset. What's the matter with you? Why can't you ever get it right?" Or whatever version of that accusatory harangue you hear in your head.

Here's the bad news:

We're conditioned to take responsibility for what we aren't doing and have no control over.

Here's the good news:

The "control" we have is to learn not to be ruled by that conversation. That's what we can take responsibility for.

Gasshō,

ch

Dear Cheri,

So, when I say something to someone and they react in anger or disappointment, that's what's going on for them? I don't have to make their reactions mean something about me?

Sincerely,

Not taking it personally

Dear Not Taking It Personally,

Exactly. None of this is "personal." It's all ego. Egocentric karmic conditioning/self-hate is like a vehicle running along a downhill track. Something set it in motion (we know not when, where, or how), and now it goes along picking up speed each time we "feed" it by giving it attention and indulging its stories.

We're practicing not feeding it! How do we not feed it? We don't give it attention, we don't indulge its stories, and we don't buy into the meaning it assigns to what happens.

That person reacting in anger or expressing disappointment is doing and saying and behaving as they are...because they are! (So Zen!) When identified with egocentric karmic conditioning/self-hate, "I" does what it does, says what it says, and behaves as it does... because it does. This same process happens in "you" and it happens in "them." In fact, it happens "to" you and it happens "to" them.
Gasshō,
ch

Dear Cheri,
    If we are all referencing what's going on in our head, is communication possible? Can I resolve something with someone else if what I say is always interpreted by their conditioning? If

22

someone says something I don't agree with, does that mean I withdraw because their ego is never going to be open to my point of view?
Sincerely,
What's the Point?

Dear What's the Point?

That's what we're doing here. We're using this content of communication, as we use all content in our lives, as a way of seeing how suffering is caused so we can drop that cause and end suffering.

Now, specifically with what you're asking: You see how what's clear to one person is very likely not clear at all to another person. Even when we think we're understanding one another, we're often not. You see that. From there we get to dismantle the conditioned belief that the other person is trying to do to us what egocentric karmic conditioning/self-hate does to us and what the voices of egocentric karmic conditioning/self-hate tell us the other person is trying to do to us.

The likelihood is great that the other person is a perfectly fine human being doing the best they can against the same nasty egocentric karmic conditioning/self-hate we're working hard to extricate ourselves from. (Getting THAT alone is worth the price of this ticket.) **Now you start practicing awareness within the content of communication.** Someone says something you "think" isn't right for you. (The quotes indicate that examining closely that information will be essential.) You use your Awareness Practice skills to explore what the person is saying. Don't let the voices in your head make you assume you know. Find out! Explore, question, reflect, be curious, choose to understand....

Gasshō,

ch

Dear Cheri,

So, if the voices are not allowed to speak, who communicates?

Sincerely,

Puzzled

Dear Puzzled,

A very good question indeed. That question arises because we don't "know" we've had any experience other than the voices of egocentric karmic conditioning/self-hate. The conditioned assumption is *deep* that ego is all there is. That's not true.

"Thinking" before we speak is a tried and true way to put conditioned mind in charge of a person's life. Conditioned mind's "thinking" process will add nothing to the moment. **Talking from ego won't either!**

So, what else is possible? That's what Awareness Practice enables us to find out.
Gasshō,
ch

Dear Cheri,

If I am not referencing the voices in my head, what would I say?
Sincerely,
Intrigued

Dear Intrigued,
    We never know—ahead of time. Life is unfolding in each moment, a completely brand new moment. If we're present, we speak from that unfolding moment. **As we get more current with attention in the present, we're increasingly able to say what's here to be said.**
    For example: When we're present we tend to notice a lot. We see a lot, hear a lot, feel a lot. Life is VERY full. It is possible to say all of what we experience, yes?
Gasshō,
ch

Dear Cheri,
    What is authentic communication?
Sincerely,
Wanting to be Authentic

Dear Wanting to Be Authentic,
    We are conditioned to believe that Life needs a "someone" to communicate, an interpreter, if you will, though it would never

be presented that way. If we consider how we're moved by words that we can feel come straight from the Heart, we know that it's possible to communicate directly with no ego interference. Our proof is every time our breath is taken away by words that travel directly from Heart to Heart.

Gasshō,

ch

Dear Cheri,
    Would you define good communication as saying what comes from the heart?
Sincerely,
Like definitions

Dear Like definitions,
    Do we need a definition? Good/bad is definitely in the dualistic realm of egocentric karmic conditioning/self-hate. To define anything is to give ego the ammunition it needs to perpetuate suffering. Perhaps we could say that "good" communication happens when ego is absent?

One of the practices of the Buddha's Eightfold Path is compassionate speech that makes for clarity. When attention is not on the conversation in conditioned mind, when we're not identified with ego, we're present, we see clearly. And from that clarity, whatever arises to say or not say is "good communication" because it comes from Goodness, Presence, Center.

Like all skills, staying present in communication takes practice. In this book, we offer ways to practice communication from presence rather than from ego-identification. Is it easy to do? No, but it is do-able, and the fact that getting HERE in this present moment ends suffering is compelling incentive for those of us attracted to ending suffering.

Don't just take our word for it.
We encourage you
to have your own direct experience.

Gasshō,
ch

Identifying Those Lying, Trickster Voices of Ego

TO BEGIN...

Here are some of the images we use in this book to illustrate the lying, trickster voices of ego that scramble communication.

 Generic ego voice - Represents any conversation in conditioned mind.

 Self-Hating ego voice - Tells you there's something wrong with you. "You just don't have what it takes."

 Critical ego voice - Has one job: to make you second-guess everything you say, do, feel, and think.

 Resistance ego voice - Says no. Never allows you to examine the possibilities that could be open to you.

Communication difficulties arise because we're deeply conditioned to believe we're present, conscious, and awake...and we're not. What we are is **identified with ego**. We see life through a veil—a bubble, let's say—and we're so accustomed to looking through it that we have no idea it's there.

With that in mind, here's a good way to bring conscious awareness to being in the bubble: When talking with someone, pay attention to how often it occurs to you to *ask them what they're thinking and feeling.*

How often do we check out whether what we're projecting onto someone, from inside our bubble, is what's really going on with them, inside their bubble? Almost never, right?

Ego voices desperately whisper, " You can't ask that!" and we go right on seeing, hearing, believing, and accepting as true our bubble-influenced perception, unable to make contact with a real person.

This ego-conversation in conditioned mind distracts us from being HERE, from being present for an exchange of information undistorted by beliefs, assumptions, opinions, positions, projections, and self-hatred. Training ourselves to recognize the conversation is the first step in removing ego's interference with communication.

Luckily for us, the conversation has a recognizable signature.

While learning to recognize when ego is "communicating," we see that ego voices tend to express:

A dualistic world view
Fear
A preoccupation with maintaining positions
A focus on "I," "me," "mine"
Judgment and criticism
Unexamined beliefs and assumptions
Feelings of victimization
A preference for isolation
A predilection for distraction
Self-hatred or "other" hatred
Arrogance
Hostility
Negativity
Fault or blame
Something wrong/not enough

(Common ego characteristics are further identified in our book *The Big Bamboozle*.)

Because we identify with ego, we believe that what it tells us is our own experience. We don't stop to question what goes on inside our head. Remember the dinner invitation from the first section?

WAIT!! Do I or don't I want to go over for dinner?!

Our ability to regain jurisdiction over what we do or don't say and feel or don't feel depends on our ability to recognize when attention is on an ego-conversation.

Something to watch for:

Ego voices speak from two angles, "I" and "you."

An extremely significant step in bringing close scrutiny to ego's shenanigans is when we are able to hear—and not believe—the "you" voice saying you should or you can't or why did you or you're not allowed to or any number of like statements. Before this, the "you" voice goes completely unnoticed, giving it the power to jerk us around through life with its criticisms. When we see how that's happening, it's all the proof we need that we are being "talked to" as opposed to "thinking." That voice is not "you," the authentic human being. That's ego!

For most people, the "I" voice makes perfect sense because it seems clear that it's "me thinking." It's not; it's ego calling itself "I." The "I" voice is harder to recognize as ego, but it's ego nonetheless. We often have an easier time recognizing it as an ego voice in situations rather than in internal conversations.

For instance, you've decided to do something that would make you feel better— exercise or meditate or stop eating sugar.

You really want this. It's is not something you came up with this morning; you've wanted this for a good long while. In fact, you've attempted it in the past, maybe lots of times. So you start. And you feel good. You're getting to do what you want. This is great. You can envision your life being different, more the way you want it to be. You're hopeful, optimistic. Then, before long, you hear (assuming you're listening), "I don't want to, I don't feel like it," and you quit your program. (We have a book by that title too, by the way.) It may not take long to remember your commitment, and you may decide to continue, but before long you'll hear it again: "I don't want to." The way that's meant to work in ego's world is for you to believe the "I" in the "don't want to" is "you." You've changed your mind. You wanted to, but now you don't.

When pointed out to those of us who have gone through that dance a few dozen (hundred) times, we can quickly see that, no, in fact, that's not me. That's the same ego voice masquerading as me that has controlled me in countless situations throughout my life.

It says I want chocolate or I don't want to exercise or I don't feel like going to bed or I don't want to work on that or I hate making phone calls or I want to play games on the computer or I don't feel like practicing or I just want to veg out or that's too hard or I want to quit or....

Recognize it? Yep, that's not a real person. That is the system we call egocentric karmic conditioning/self-hate that's controlling people's lives because *people don't know it's there and don't know what it's doing.*

Overstating the significance of seeing this is impossible. We can't step free of its grip on our lives if we identity with it and believe we are it. And, needless to say, it's also controlling communication.

Let's practice recognizing ego conversations. (This is not a comprehensive list; keep looking out for additions.)

EXERCISE ✏️

When you're stopped from saying something, what stops you? Is it:

-- Fear?
I'm afraid of what will happen to me if I say something. What if I say the wrong thing?
-- Unexamined Beliefs & Assumptions?
They know what I mean. It would be condescending to explain something so obvious.
-- Judgment? If you're too stupid to hear what I'm saying, I can't help you.
-- Arrogance? I don't have time to explain myself to people who aren't going to understand anyway.
-- Blame? She isn't even trying to get it.
-- Focus on me? It's so obvious to me!
-- Victim? If you loved me, you would know.
-- Paranoia? I can't trust any of them.
-- Hostility? It's none of their business, they don't need to know, let them figure it out.
-- Add your own:

Notice what prompts you to say something you later regret. Is it:
-- Self-righteousness? I have a valid point of view. They need to hear it!
-- Arrogance? Of course I'm right. I have to bring them around to my perspective.
-- Feeling Victimized? He needs to know what he's doing that's making my life miserable.
-- Focus on me? I can't stand it anymore. You need to hear me!
-- Add your own:

Notice how whether you say something or not, the voices of self-hate usually chime in:
-- Why can't you ever say what you mean?
-- That was not skillful!
-- I wish I could take that back.
-- Why did you say that?
-- You never mean what you say.
---- Add your own:

Let's look more closely at ego signatures in communication.

-- You versus Me (a dualistic world view)

It's helpful to keep in mind that the ego-maintaining conversation in the head is there to maintain ego, PERIOD. It's not going to pursue activities that conflict with its agenda. To preserve an illusion of being other than, separate from everyone and everything, the conversation in the head cannot be egalitarian; it has to be dualistic. The world of ego is the world of opposites. If I'm to be right, you have to be wrong. If I'm wrong it's because you're right. That's the only way to maintain a sense of "me" distinct from everyone else. How can I feel separate, and different and "me" except as different from the "other"?

Dear Cheri,

   Each time I defend my position
I have a falling out with my partner.
If I am willing to let go my position, then it's
more likely we get to an understanding.
Sincerely,
Position/Positionless,

Dear Position/Positionless,
   That's a key insight! Congratulations. It's
exactly as you laid out. Egocentric karmic
conditioning/self-hate IS an imaginary world of
dualities. The first duality for just about
everyone is "me and you." Except it's actually
"me or you." Because ego is an illusion of being
separate from Life (as preposterous as that is
once we realize it), ego makes a duality of "me
(ego) or Life." It's silly but conditioned people
have been bamboozled into believing it deeply,
and, as we know, we humans can be brainwashed
into believing anything—and have been! Drop
ego and there's just what is so. "Us." "We."
   Thisherenow with nothing left out.
Gasshō,
ch

Dear Cheri,

I am looking at my interactions with a colleague who bores me. I'm not interested in talking to her but I have to out of politeness. I try to avoid her if possible. What do I do about this problem person?

Sincerely,

Bored

Dear Bored,

Are you sure she is the problem? Are you sure the problem isn't with the conversation in your head? Have you noticed that when you're with this person all your attention is going to the conversation in conditioned mind, attending to what it says about how you feel, what that means, what you should do, etc.?

You're being told: She's boring. I can't stand being around her. Pretend not to see her. Perhaps followed by "You are so judgmental."

That conversation is running the show. It's framing your world: "You versus her." If you weren't constantly listening to and believing it, you'd be living in a different reality. You're not experiencing the world as it is; you're experiencing ego as it is.

Ego says "boring" when nothing is reflecting it the way it wants to be reflected. "Bored" will make a person hop to and give attention to ego like nothing else. Ego's focus becomes getting you to try to sort out what is true about "her" and is the source of your misery. That's its strategy to ensure "you" never realize that the problem is not with what *triggers* ego, it's with egocentric karmic conditioning/ self-hate itself.

Gasshō,

ch

Dear Cheri,

My communication problems happen with authority figures. The intensity of physical sensations when I'm around anyone I perceive has more power than I do, shuts me down. I resent how I'm treated but am unable to leave.

Sincerely,

Shut Down

Dear Shut Down,

Nothing sets off hysteria in conditioned mind quite like the notion of "authority figure." I hear *with great regularity*, "I don't do well with authority figures." The reason we don't do well with *external* authority figures is that

EGO
SUPREME
COMMANDER

they run into the *real* "authority" figure in our lives: ego. Ego is able to play the role it does because it has established itself as the *supreme* authority. When ego encounters someone who might exert more influence than it does, the battle is on. The conversation in the head turns to judgment, suspicion, and case building. Evidence is being gathered that will ultimately result in the fall of the (external) authority figure, leaving the real "authority" safely in charge of the human being.

The other side of the issue (in the dualistic world of ego there's always the other side) is projecting authority onto another and then allowing that person to work in tandem with an abusive, self-hating voice in the head. I pick a partner who treats me in the same punishing way I was treated as a child. Believing I "deserve" that treatment, I allow that person to play the external voice that reinforces "my" internal voice. Even though I'm miserable (likely *because* I'm miserable,) I will shut down, hide my upset, and redouble my efforts not to "get in trouble" again.

The way out of this dilemma is to overthrow the authority of the voice in your head. How? Stop allowing the conversation in conditioned mind to be the boss.

Gasshō,

ch

Dear Cheri,

I feel crushed when someone disagrees with me. It's as if what I said or did is being dismissed. It's actually worse. I'm being dismissed for not working hard enough or doing a good enough job. How should I be practicing with this?

Sincerely,

Crushed

Dear Crushed,

The practice is to stop making everything about "me." Stop making personal what is not personal. If our relationship weren't about "me," I'd be interested in your perspective. I'd want to know how you see things and why. I'd want to know what makes you think that. How do you get there? I'd want to get to know you.

All of those "ego assumptions" (being dismissed, not working hard enough, not doing a good job) are utterly bogus and exist only to keep ego at center stage all the time. If you work hard enough and do a good enough job will people not disagree with you? The first place to look might be what you've been conditioned to call "disagreement" and what "disagreement" means.

Remember, in ego's dualistic world, for ego to exist "you" will always have to be an issue for "me."

Gasshō,

ch

Dear Cheri,
   What do I do when I find myself in a conversation with someone who is mean and manipulative? I don't want to accuse them of that, but that's how they're being. I don't say anything and then feel bad for not standing up for myself.
Sincerely,
A pushover

Dear A pushover,
   How would I know if someone is being mean and manipulative? Listening to conditioned mind, I can quickly and easily judge that you're being mean or manipulative, but whose head did that appear in and whose mouth would it come out of? Mine. I'm the only one having the "mean and manipulative" experience!
   As we begin to watch conditioned mind, as we see what it's projecting, we begin to realize this stuff (these labels, judgments, beliefs, assumptions, opinions) isn't me, and it isn't you either. It's conditioned mind. It's ego. Most of us in relationship with other human beings have a TON of looking inward to do before we even

think of turning attention to what the "other" might be doing.
Gasshō,
ch

--Something Wrong & Feeling Bad

A favorite suffering-causing tactic of the voices is convincing us that "whatever you do is wrong."
-- Say something and what you said is wrong.
-- Don't say something and not saying something is wrong.
-- Saying too little is wrong.
-- Saying too much is wrong.

We fall for this "pillar of suffering" because we've accepted as fact the idea that "there is a way to be." Once we're convinced there's a "right way" in every

situation, we'll look to conditioned mind to know what that right way is.

Sadly, the system we're looking to for direction is the same system that will say we did the wrong thing after we do what it tells us to do!

We're trained to believe that the voice telling us what to do and how to do it and what not to do and how not to do it is there to take care of us, is on our side, is helping us to be a "good person." As we watch, we realize that if that system were on our side we would hear "that's right, good job," and we would get regular assurance that being a good person is not dependent on meeting performance standards. But that's not what happens, and we can see that constantly hearing "you did it wrong" makes it difficult for a person to realize "I'm a good person."

We call the voice—the one telling you what's wrong with you, what you should have done, how incompetent, stupid, and unskillful you are—the voice of self-hate.

It's essential to see that the negative conversation in conditioned mind is not

there because you're doing something wrong or there's something wrong with you. It talks unceasingly so that you'll never take your eyes and attention off of it. Giving attention to the self-hating force that makes you feel bad guarantees that no authentic communication ever takes place.

As we practice with communication, or anything else, the first voice we have to stop listening to and believing is the voice that makes us feel bad.

For more on getting past self-hate, you might enjoy *There Is Nothing Wrong with You: Going Beyond Self-Hate*.

Dear Cheri,
I am afraid I'll say the wrong thing at work and annoy my colleagues. I wish there was a way to check out what I'm going to say before I say it so I won't have to face the sensations in my body when I try to speak. I

want to get past this fear, to be indifferent to people's opinions of me. So what if I get it wrong?
Sincerely,
Wanting to get it right

Dear Wanting to get it right,
    The system that you're looking to for approval is never going to give it to you. You'll always be wrong if you consult those ego voices in your head. They judge you and project judgment of you onto your colleagues. You have no way of knowing whether your colleagues find your communication annoying. No matter how they respond, as long as you reference that voice in your head, you'll be told that what you said was wrong. With every consultation, the story of what's wrong with you is reinforced, and each previous story is simply proof that "you'll never get it right."

The only way we can get past the fear is by ceasing to reference that voice and by not looking to it for an assessment of our communications.

Gasshō,

ch

Dear Cheri,

I was appalled when I lost it at a family gathering and yelled "I hate you all." I can usually keep it together, but I've noticed that when I don't get to say what I want to say and don't feel heard, I often explode and say something unskillful. Then I feel awful.

Sincerely,

Explosive

Dear Explosive,

What likely happened is something like this: You have been listening to a conversation in your head—probably unaware it's going on—about "everything that's wrong." You have something to say but you can't because you don't have the right to say it, you can't say it skillfully, your input is irrelevant anyway, they don't care, they don't want to hear what you have to say....

The conversation is upsetting and you're more and more riled. There's an enormous amount of energy being generated and the sensations in the body are ricocheting around. Finally, everything builds to an intolerable level and you're "told" you "can't stand it." At this point you hear and feel "I hate everyone" and you say it out loud.

That's not you talking, that's ego.

Then, there's probably a rush of new sensations that mean how wrong that was, how you can't feel and say things like that. What a bad, wrong, horrible person you are. You're blamed for what ego did, you accept the blame, and feel appalled at having "lost it."

Ego got its way and say, and you got silenced and blamed.

Gasshō,

ch

Dear Cheri,

I realize that when I communicate with someone, I'm expecting a certain response, a particular outcome. I want to be liked, loved, respected, understood, and seen in a positive light. If I don't receive a signal from the other person that they've understood me or like me, I feel I have failed in my communication. I end up feeling disconsolate. How can I improve my communication skills so I can get the result I'm looking for?

Sincerely,
Disconsolate

Dear Disconsolate,

Egocentric karmic conditioning/self-hate tricks people with all sorts of bamboozles. The one you describe is a popular one: If X, then Y. If you behave in certain ways, *then* you'll get the result you want. Well, actually, no. You never will get that result because the self-hate setting the scene is setting it precisely so that you **won't** get what you want.

And the cruelest part of the whole mess is that without looking to egocentric karmic conditioning/self-hate to direct your behavior, you'd very likely realize you already have the result you want. People, not all but some people, probably do like you, love you, respect you, and see you in a positive light. No shenanigans by ego are necessary to make that happen; ego's involvement is an attempt to prevent you from *realizing* that's already happening so that you will feel bad and stay in a conversation with it.

Gasshō,

ch

-- Opposition/Negation

We often talk about ego as "no" to Life's "yes." The moment unfolds. Ego's reaction is "No, I don't like that, I don't want that, I don't feel like it, I don't want to, I won't." Ego resistance can also take the form of, "Don't do that, you don't want to, you don't feel like it, that's not for you, you can't, you shouldn't, you'd better not." Whatever form they take, all negative voices are ego.

Dear Cheri,
    I suffer intensely because I cannot say no. I find myself doing things I don't want to do, feeling stressed about keeping my commitments because I often prioritize other people's needs over mine. If I say no, I feel bad. So I'd rather say yes. But when I do say yes, and then miss all the things I have to do, I still feel awful.
Sincerely,
Can't Say No

Dear Can't Say No,
    The trouble we have with "no" only applies to saying no "outside."
    Someone asks me for something. I'm conditioned to be polite, be nice, be agreeable,

57

and get along with others. I'm hearing a loud "no!" inside my head, which now has to compete with the "do the right thing" programmed ego reaction. Here's the piece it's important for us to consider: If there weren't a forceful no from egocentric karmic conditioning/self-hate inside, I could happily say yes to someone else's request. If the conditioned no weren't colliding with the "how I should be" message, I could say either yes or no, depending on the moment.

We really have to go beyond the obvious for this one. I *deeply* believe the no I hear inside my head is what's true for me. I also *deeply* believe I need to "do the right thing in order to be a good person."

Here's the big question: What if the no I hear in my head is simply there to set up the conflict between "what I want" and "how I should be"?

When we go up against ego—saying yes when we're being told we want to say no or saying no when we're being told we should say yes—we're trained to feel bad. We're meant to believe we feel bad about the content (saying yes or no when we "should have" said no or yes), but the feeling bad never comes from the particular circumstances. As we watch the process, we see how we're being set up to feel bad—regardless.

For example: You ask me if I can help you move on the weekend. I say yes because you're my friend, I love you, and I do want to help you. But I don't want to. I have other plans for the weekend and am really excited about them. I feel good that I'm going to help you, but I feel bad that I don't really want 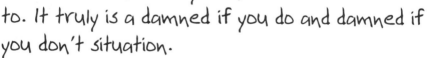 to. It truly is a damned if you do and damned if you don't situation.

In communication, as with all other content in Life, all roads lead to feeling bad as long as we're looking to egocentric karmic conditioning/self-hate to find out "how I'm doing."

Gasshō,

ch

-- Opposition/Negation continued

As we observe the various forms of no with which the conversation in conditioned mind meets the yes of each moment unfolding, we begin to see the role of egocentric karmic conditioning/self-hate in conflict. Avoiding being obvious in its controlling manipulations, ego maneuvers to remain below the level of conscious awareness. "Avoiding conflicts" is a popular way for ego to maintain an oppositional position against Life, while obscuring the ways its narrative is keeping a person in a constant state of conflict.

Dear Cheri,
        I am conflict averse. When I look at that a little further, I see that I don't know how to communicate when someone has an opposing point of view. I don't enjoy debate and so I just don't say anything.

Sincerely,
Tongue-Tied at Opposition

Dear Tongue-Tied at Opposition,
The illusion of being a "me" that is separate from the rest of Life is maintained by the assumption that "I" am the subject to which all else is object. I am this; everything else is that. We can also say, I am *this*. Everything else is *not this*. This very orientation is one of conflict. True, the relationship doesn't always have the contention, discord, hostility, or clashing we think of with conflict, though it often does.
The real conflict is due to identification with ego. Identified with ego, I am one way and you're not that way. Ego has turned us into opposites.

-- I'm giving, generous, and supportive in relationships, but I can't ask for what I want because what I ask for might be refused. (I'm generous. They're not.)

-- I can't show up as I am and communicate who I am because I'll be rejected. (They're authentic. I'm not.)

-- They don't care about you, you can't ask for that, they won't like you. (I'm caring. They're not.)

-- They say what they want to say clearly. But I get so tongue-tied. (They're good communicators. I'm not.)

-- What you have to say is really important but nobody wants to hear it. (I listen. They don't.)

-- Forget it. They don't understand and they don't want to. (I'm understanding. They're not.)

When we're identified with ego (illusion of a separate self), everything else is viewed as "not me." We *feel* this as rejection and separation. It's possible to step back and recognize that it's the ego identification, not the other people, that is the source of the conflict.

In exploring the topic of communication it becomes clear that most people are hiding who they are, what they feel, what they think, and what is so for them. The injunctions in

conditioned mind not to be "real" (it may never be stated, but that's the message) are so strong that enormous amounts of energy are tied up in dissembling and pretending.
Gasshō
ch

-- Judgment

People report being afraid of saying something because they feel constantly judged. People are right! We're always being judged, but not by "those people out there." The ego voices of self-hate are constantly judging us and convincing us that others feel about us what the self-hating voices are saying *to us about us.* The truth of it is, we don't know what anyone else is thinking or feeling. They may or may not be judging us but all we know for sure is what the voices are telling us. Ego is safe because we're not allowed to question the voices say.

Dear Cheri,

My problem seems to be my inability to communicate what I feel when I'm being criticized. My boss is really critical. He seems to keep it together for a while, something sets him off, and he starts criticizing. I find this really upsetting. I don't think he should criticize me. I don't deserve it and I think it's wrong.

Sincerely,
Feeling Criticized

Dear Feeling Criticized,

If not for the conversation in the head making a case against the boss and this "wrong" behavior, it would be obvious that criticizing is just what this guy does. If I don't take it personally, I can feel sorry for him that he gets so upset or happy for him that he's so expressive. In any case it has nothing to do with me. Egocentric karmic conditioning/self-hate wants to make everything about "me." Not the "me," the human being who is embodied and goes to work, but the "me" that is an imaginary voice in the head.

For your consideration: Do you realize you're criticizing your boss for criticizing you? That's an important piece to catch. When I feel "justified," I'm not criticizing, I'm just pointing out what he's doing and that it's wrong. That's what he's doing too. What's likely going on with him? He's hearing a story in his head that makes him start criticizing. In that story he's justified. He's right. The criticism is warranted.

As awareness practitioners we can choose for it to end with us. When we feel judged or criticized, we don't need to judge and criticize in return.

Gasshō,

ch

-- Unexamined Beliefs and Assumptions

The beliefs and assumptions that operate us are largely unseen. Perhaps our greatest difficulty is the unquestioned assumption that we know what's going on. We assume we're conscious. We assume our experience is the result of what's happening in this moment. We assume our projections are accurate readings of people and circumstances. In fact, our assumptions are so deep and so unquestioned that it rarely occurs to us to find out if our version of reality matches that of anyone else. This explains a lot of communication issues!

Dear Cheri,

My problem is how other people communicate! I am a clear, precise, direct communicator. I feel frustrated and angry when other people beat

around the bush in a vague, noncommittal way.
Why can't people simply get to the point?
Sincerely,
A Frustrated Communicator

Dear Frustrated Communicator,
    When we're looking out through our
conditioned beliefs and assumptions we see
what we're conditioned to see. We project that
what we're experiencing is "true." So, I "know"
what clear, precise, and direct communication is
and I'm clearly meeting the standard for that
kind of communication.
    We stumble over the notion that others
might not share our definition of clear, precise
and direct. For example, if I'm talking with
someone who above all else values kindness and
defines kindness as gentle and non-
confrontational, my clear, precise, and direct
will not only not be valued, it may be seen as
hostile or aggressive.
Gasshō,
ch

Dear Cheri,

I am often dumbfounded when I approach someone with something fairly innocuous and they are rude! I want to lash out. Is it wrong to expect people to be polite?

Sincerely,
Common Courtesy Please!

Dear Common Courtesy Please!

It is the nature of assumption to be unexamined rather than being in the front of conscious awareness. I'm polite because that's just how a decent person should be, and I assume others will be polite as well. It's upsetting to run afoul of unconscious beliefs and assumptions. We tend to feel bad when we, or others, don't behave as a person "should."

Listening to conditioned mind's directions for how not to be rude, not to hurt someone's feelings, not to rock any boats, not to intrude, not to be overbearing, or not to make a situation worse is ego's technique for staying in control. Its primary injunction is: Above all, don't make yourself or anyone else uncomfortable.

When our unexamined beliefs and assumptions are challenged, we have the opportunity to explore how they control us. What might arise as a response if we're not reacting to a belief that is being challenged by someone's "lack of politeness"?
Gasshō,
ch

Dear Cheri,
I work hard to communicate clearly and kindly. I avoid communicating difficult information out of fear of disapproval, which builds resentment. I'm then prone to blow up, feel bad, and try to re-earn approval. I sometimes over-communicate to make sure I'm understood, which can be controlling and a turn off for other people.
Sincerely,
Trying to be a better communicator

Dear Trying to be a better communicator,

Do you communicate about your communication? In other words, do you say to people, "I'm working hard to communicate clearly and kindly here," before you communicate? To make that your first point of clarity? Do you let people know that you perceive particular information as "difficult to receive" and therefore avoid communicating? Do you reveal to people that your tendency to "over-communicate" comes from a desire for them to understand you and not feel bad about what you're communicating?

Do you see what I'm asking? We go around in our own little "reality," assuming everyone else is in that reality with us. We know they're not but we operate as if they are. It can be helpful to reveal what's going on with us rather than allowing ego's assumptions to run the show. Dogs roll over to  reveal their underbelly to communicate "I'm not a threat," and just about everyone loves them!

When we fall for an ego assumption along the lines of "I wish other people tried as hard to be considerate," we step into a very large ego-built hole of believing we know what's going on with other people. We don't. Someone could be trying with everything they have to be considerate, and if they're not doing it in a way that meets "my" conditioned standards, they're going to be written off as inconsiderate by that voice in my head.

Gasshō,

ch

-- Fear

Notice the number of times you don't want to say something because you're afraid. Afraid of what? Afraid of offending someone? Afraid of disapproval? Afraid of judgment? Afraid of conflict? Afraid of making someone uncomfortable? If I'm identified with fear, I'm guaranteed not to be present and available to what might be helpful for me to say or for the other person to hear.

Fear is the best way to control someone, and the voices of ego/self-hate excel at making people afraid. What we're truly afraid of is what the voices will do to us if we don't do exactly what they say. (*The Fear Book* is our book on, well, fear!)

Dear Cheri,
    I don't say what occurs to me to say because I'm afraid of disapproval. If someone disapproves of me, it means that they don't like me and I'm afraid of not being liked. These fears don't feel "made up." They feel real. Fear causes me to censor what I say, frame it carefully, and scan for feedback. Are you saying that fear is also a conversation in my head?
Gasshō,
Afraid of Disapproval

Dear Afraid of Disapproval,
    Yes. I am saying that "fear" is a result of listening to the voices in your head. What you're feeling and calling fear is the ego conversation telling you the stories you will believe, stories designed to frighten you. If you never heard inside your head that there is something wrong with you, that people don't like you, that unless you're approved of by someone else you're not likeable, you would never be aware of disapproval or dislike. Please stop for a bit and consider that.
Gasshō,
ch

Dear Cheri,
Sometimes I feel scared to share how I feel in case I'm rejected or in case it's used against me. I keep quiet until things look clearer. Sometimes that can leave less time for something that turns out to be lovely when I find the courage to communicate.
Sincerely,
Running out of Time

Dear Running out of Time,

   That "scared" is nothing more than egocentric karmic conditioning/self-hate exerting its control over you. As you continue to watch, you'll realize the only "rejection" you get and the only "using against you" happens inside your head. The voices get you to hang back—robbing others of the pleasure of you—and then when you're finally allowed to participate, time runs out.

   First job is to watch
   how seldom anything "bad"
   comes from outside of you
   and how often the "bad" is in
   a conversation in your head.

   Even if someone were to yell at me "You're stupid and ugly and I hate you," it would be a problem only if the voices in my head made it a problem. Without believing a "yeah, you're stupid and ugly and people hate you" self-hating voice in my head, I would just feel sorry for such a misguided person!
Gasshō,
ch

Dear Cheri,

It's hard for me to give information to someone if I project that it would make them feel bad. I'm so afraid of hurting someone's feelings that I don't say what needs to be said. This happens a lot around dating. I just can't tell someone that I don't want to see them again.

Sincerely,
Nice

Dear Nice,

We don't actually hurt someone's feelings. When we're here, present, and not attending to and bamboozled by the meaning-making-machine in our head, information is simply Information. It's only when that information is taken personally and interpreted to mean something about "me" that it results in being "hurt."

When not identified with ego, it's easy to see that there are lots of very fine human beings that we don't want to date. Lots. And there's roughly the same number of human beings who don't want to date us. If we realize that's all that's going on, we can deliver the information in the same kind, nonjudgmental way we can approach everything else in life. Every choice we make is our choice. You don't feel the need, I hope, to "explain why" you drive the car you drive or wear the clothes you wear or eat what you eat for fear of upsetting or offending someone.

We can be skillful in how we deliver information, but it's always good to realize that when what is offered is taken personally, it's because what's receiving the information is the conditioning that makes you, the other person, and the circumstances "wrong."

Gasshō,

ch

Practicing Disidentification

Disidentification is the movement out of conditioned mind and into the awareness that enables us to observe ego rather than talking and acting from it. To scrutinize ego can be fun and illuminating. The following questions allow us to put the ego conversation under a microscope and catch on to what's going on in conditioned mind.

-- What are the voices saying? (Even if you don't hear words, there is a meaning that's being thought, felt or sensed.)
-- What is being projected? (What do you think others are thinking and feeling?)
-- What beliefs and assumptions are operating? (What seems "obviously true"?)
-- Is there any self-hate? (Am I, or anyone, being judged and criticized on any level about anything?)
-- "Who" is speaking? (Which one of the many, many aspects of the personality is in control of

my thought processes and vocal cords right now?)

Here is an example:

Bill reports: I find myself not saying something because I'm afraid. It often happens in a meeting at work. I'm listening to the discussion and realize I have pertinent information. Then the moment passes. Most often, something happens and I realize that if I had said something, a mistake could have been avoided. Then I kick myself for not having said something.

That's Bill caught in a story. If Bill put what was actually happening during that meeting under an awareness microscope and asked the question, "What were the voices saying?" he might report something like this:

I'm in a meeting and realize I have information to share. At this point the voices say:

"Well, the information may not be useful."

"What if I say something, it misses the point, and I sound like a fool?"

"Just wait. Don't say anything yet. You can always add something later if it seems appropriate."

I realize that my attention is on the should I or shouldn't I going on in my head and I miss what's going on in the room! I lose track of what's being said. Then the voices say:

"You're missing what others are saying."

"Should I jump in? What if the moment has passed?"

"What if someone else has made the point I'd be making?"

"Better not say anything."

Later I learn the decision that was made had disastrous results. The conversation then is:

"Why don't you speak up?"

"Why is it that you miss every chance you have of offering something helpful?"

"If you had said something, you could have prevented those disastrous results."

"Curses. If only I had spoken up!"

As Bill jots down these voices, he might notice some

unexamined beliefs and assumptions that are part of his conditioning...

-- It's possible to make a mistake.
-- There will be time to correct this.
-- It's not appropriate to ask someone to repeat what they said.
-- It's foolish to make the same point someone else made.

He can then look to see if what's going on in his head is really *his* experience. He might notice that ego is making all kinds of projections, none of which he actually knows to be true. For example:

"They won't think what I have to say is appropriate."

"They won't value my input."

And, of course, he can see the self-hate that makes him feel bad!

"It's your fault.

"You could have prevented it."

As we train ourselves to "hear" what the ego voices are saying by putting them under a microscope and becoming familiar with the language and the programming, we will register when attention is on a conversation and realize it's ego talking. In that moment of realization we're present, we've disidentified. Now a window for authentic communication is open.

getting Clear
Recording & Listening
-R/L for short-

Enormous amounts of suffering happen because we're conditioned with "don't say anything."

Enormous amounts of suffering also happen because we're conditioned to identify with ego and let it do our talking for us rather than being present.

In either case, whether ego voices are shutting us up or goading us on, our underlying belief is that saying or not saying something will solve the problem. It never does. What we need is a way to sort out what's really going on for us *BEFORE* we attempt to communicate with someone else. We need to take time to discern what is so for us and what is being distorted by the conversation in conditioned mind.

Enter Recording and Listening practice.

-- Recording & Listening helps to get some distance from the voices.

Recording is a safe way to say whatever we want to say without inhibition, censure, or fear of recrimination. Recording what's going on for me, what I'm *not allowed* to say, plus what I'm afraid I *will* say, creates distance from the conversation in the head. Instead of being controlled by the voices that either stop me from saying something or goad me into saying something I'll later regret, I can transfer the contents of conditioned mind onto a recording device.

-- Recording and Listening allows us to feel heard.

People often feel "no one listens to me." Through R/L practice, we begin to realize that "I don't listen to myself because I've been trained to listen to ego voices in conditioned mind instead of listening to me." Really *hearing* me begins to change dramatically my relationship with myself and with everyone else.

Everyone *wants* to be heard; R/L is how we can be heard.

Practice: RECORD

Turn on a recorder and record some of the things you've not been allowed to say, the things you hear in your head over and over again but are not allowed to say aloud.

Watch *how* the voices attempt to stop you from recording. Do they second-guess ("that's not really true..."), judge ("you're just being a self-centered personal pity party"), dismiss ("you just make this stuff up so you can be the center of the universe"), heckle ("I hate the sound of your voice")? Or maybe you hear some of ego's other favorites: "This is stupid," "a waste of time," "all the proof you need that there really is something wrong with you."

Practice: LISTEN

Recognizing that chatter for what it is—ego resisting having you do something that *will* free you from its grip of suffering—listen to what you recorded. Hint: Watch how the voices try to interfere with your ability to listen.

With practice we can train ourselves simply to listen to the recording, be present to what's going on for the person who made the recording, and be aware of but not give attention to the voices of the ego. Instead of believing that what we're hearing in our head is true, we have the opportunity to sort out what is so and how it's being scrambled by the ego scrambler. Identifying the messages, beliefs, projections, and assumptions reveals what is conditioning, what is ego yammering, and what is truly going on for the human being.

As we practice in this way we begin to get the distance necessary to realize "I'm not saying those things. I'm *hearing* them, but I'm not *speaking* them." This is an essential step in seeing that what's going on inside conditioned mind is exactly that—conditioning. It's programmed. It was programmed in when we were children. It's the conclusions of a child's mind trying to make sense of an incomprehensible world, added to and morphed through adolescence, and solidified in adulthood. It may have been part of surviving as a child, but it has no place in an adult's life.

No place.

Whatsoever.

The Mentor

When we attempt to communicate, most of us are looking to be heard, accepted, validated, encouraged, appreciated, and consoled when appropriate. Sometimes a partner, friend, or family member can be with us exactly as we want them to. But more often than not, however much someone might want to, they can't.

Why is this? Just about everyone, ourselves included, is being interfered with by ego voices pretty much all the time, and despite best efforts the input and output signals get distorted.

The very, very good news is that we not only don't need to be stuck there in the suffering of distorted signals, we have a source of Unconditional Love and Acceptance surprisingly close at hand, always available, ready to listen and respond. This source of wisdom, love, and compassion, always accessible, always kind, and always on our side is the

Intelligence That Animates. We call it the Mentor.

If this sounds improbable, we ask you to consider this: Have you ever offered words of wisdom, encouragement, and comfort to a friend who is having a hard time and then been surprised that those words came from you? You didn't realize what you were saying until you heard the words, felt their rightness, and saw them "land" for your friend. In that moment, you *knew* how perfect the message was, and you also knew that you didn't think it up. It just came *through* you.

That's what
we're talking about.

The Mentor is the centered awareness that observes and acknowledges conditioned mind without a self-hating reaction to it. We resolve what's going on for us by talking it over with the Mentor *first*. When we can "communicate with the Mentor," communicating with other people becomes much less fraught.

Ready to try it? (If you're getting a lot of push back here, don't think you're alone.) This simple practice removes ego's ability to control you, and, yes, ego knows that. *That's* why there's so much resistance. If you're experiencing some of that resistance, please consider this: Would anyone who cares about you discourage you from trying *anything* that might assist you? Of course not. We can assure you that no one has ever died or even been mildly injured from doing this practice. If you try it and it's not working, you can always quit and go back to listening full-time to hateful voices in your head. So, here we go:

1. Hold the recorder in your right hand and talk as you would to a close friend. Without censoring, express what you're feeling.

Say everything you ever wanted about what you're going through. (This often takes courage, even though no one else is listening!)

2. When you feel you've said it all, stop the recorder. Breathe. Sit with the experience. Then, holding the recorder in your left hand, listen to the recording, giving it your full attention. Really listen. (If you got distracted and didn't listen closely, listen again.)
3. Keeping the recorder in the left hand, record whatever occurs to you that could assist and comfort the person you just listened to.
4. Listen to the recording you just made.

This is called the Two-Handed Recording Exercise. Another way to describe this exercise:

We talk.
Compassion listens.
We feel heard
Compassion speaks.
We listen.
We receive clear, compassionate information.
This exercise is a powerful support for authentic communication. It allows us to give to ourselves and to receive for ourselves what we desire from communications with others.

-- It gives us "someone" to talk with, someone always available, always interested and on our side.
-- It lets us feel heard.
-- It lets us sort out what's really going on for us.
-- It allows us to recognize ego interference and to stop believing ego is who we are.
-- It gives us clarity about what we want to say versus what ego wants to say.

We encourage you to keep repeating the Two-Handed Recording Exercise. What you're doing is assisting the only human being you'll ever know with this level of intimacy to end suffering.

It's the best thing
we can ever do,
for ourselves and for the world.

How the Mentor Assists in Communication

You are told that:
-- it's best not to say anything.
-- it's best to give voice to displeasure, worry, dissatisfaction, resentment, anger.
-- no one wants to listen to what you want to say.
-- you've repeatedly failed to get your point across.
-- you can't find anyone who will validate or understand what you feel.
-- you don't know why you're feeling the way you do.
-- you must find out why you feel the way you do.
-- no one shares your happiness, enthusiasm, and excitement, and you watch that lovely energy fade away as you try to communicate it.
-- you "lost it" and now must feel bad.
-- add your own

     In these instances of the ego scrambler in action, pick up the recorder and practice talking things over with the Mentor. Explore what's going on

SCRAMBLER
EGO

for you. See what is so for you. Then, when you have said it all, heard it all, *felt* it all, look to see if there is anything that it is necessary to say to another person. Talk that over with the Mentor.

If there is something you want to say to the other person, practice two things:

1. Rehearse with the recorder.

Let the Mentor remind you that you're doing Awareness Practice, and that Life is a great big workshop in which we get to move from suffering to freedom. There are no mistakes; there's only seeing, learning, realizing, letting go, and accepting.

2. Review with the recorder.

After saying to the person what you talked over with the Mentor, commit to coming back to the recorder to explore how it went. Let the R/L practice assist you not to let ego do the review. If there's something you need to see, that clarity will drop in for you through insight. Clarity will never arrive through a conversation in conditioned mind. NEVER.

Feeling Understood

Dear Cheri,

    My challenge is in communication with my husband of 40 years. With practice, I feel stronger and surer in most areas of my life, but in my marriage I find myself misunderstood and feeling like I have to defend myself. My reaction is to shut down to avoid conflict. I'm feeling very detached and wondering if I have the right to expect things to change.

Sincerely,

Feeling detached

Dear Feeling detached,

    Isn't it interesting that we expect to be understood and validated by our loved ones? I sometimes wonder if this expectation is perpetuated because we're oblivious to how often we miss the mark with those loved ones.

This can leave us assuming that most of the time we're on target, while they are almost always off. With Awareness Practice, first we look to see if our assumption is true; next, we might look to see if that need to feel understood can be met without expecting someone else to meet it.

This is one of those places where a Recording and Listening practice comes in handy. It is helpful to practice with the Mentor before delivering difficult communication in intimate relationship. Say everything you need to say, expressing yourself fully. Then, when you are with your husband, you're not looking to express or to be understood. You already have that; expressing and being understood are complete. Now you're just delivering information.

Conditioned voices will say this is unfair, that you shouldn't be treated that way, he should listen to and understand you, but those voices are not interested in your well-being—or his. It will be interesting to see if that "stronger and surer" begins to enter the relationship as you look less to conditioned mind's stories and become less dependent on (ego's version of) his approval. This might just free him up as well, though we can't do what we do in the hopes of getting something we want from someone else.

Gasshō,

ch

True Relating

Dear Cheri,

Communication is challenging when "I" feel disconnected from everything. I want to relate to others and feel connected, but I don't feel connected to anything, including me. Do I have to fix that first?

Sincerely,

Disconnected

Dear Disconnected,

Yes, you do! First, we must be at one with "ourselves." The Buddha taught that we have one person to save—our "self." We can save the human incarnation, release it from the grip of egocentric karmic conditioning/self-hate, and return it to Unconditional Love and Acceptance. That's what we're practicing.

And this is what Recording and Listening practice assists with.

> You get to develop a relationship
> with the you that isn't
> the "I" of ego.

Practice making recordings as you go about your day, recording what you love, what you're grateful for, what you did, what's challenging for you. As you listen to your recordings, get a sense of who that human being is.

As you practice R/L, you will find increased ability to "stay connected with you" (disidentified from ego). As that happens you can be—and *feel*—connected as you relate to another person through communication.

Gasshō,

ch

Becoming a Friend

Dear Cheri,

    I fail in most communications and I have few friends as a result. The ensuing loneliness and belief that I lack the friend-making communication skills others have are scary.

Sincerely,
Alone & Friendless

Dear Alone & Friendless,

    No. Listening to and believing those voices is scary! You do not fail in communications. You're *told* you fail to ensure attention is on the stories of failure in your head rather than on the person you want to connect with.

    You have everything you need to be a great friend. We all do. First, we must learn to be that great friend with ourselves. Once that's accomplished, we find we have lots of opportunities to be that great friend with others.

    Developing an R/L

practice will allow you to be your own best friend. Having that relationship removes just about all the weapons ego uses to hold us hostage. We're now HERE, present, interested in Life, which includes lots of people to be interested in. Being interested in folks is a very friendly, likeable trait. Soon there will be no room in your inner circle for hateful voices calling you a failure.

Gasshō,

ch

A Love We Cannot Lose

Dear Cheri,

I cannot say what's going on for me because I'm afraid I will lose my partner's love. It's irrational I know but the fear is real. I've left a number of relationships because I find myself literally suffocating emotionally. Using the recorder has been helpful because I can now say what I feel to somebody! But the fear of losing love is still there.

Sincerely,

Afraid to Lose Love

Dear Afraid to Lose Love,

A love we can lose is not love. A clearer way to depict that is, "A love we can lose is not LOVE." If we don't have Unconditional Love, we don't have love at all. Are we likely to receive Unconditional Love from another human being? No. Which brings us to what all our spiritual heroes encourage us to consider:

Only we can find Unconditional Love
in and for ourselves.

When we have that, when we know the LOVE that IS, we know that's what we ARE and what everything IS. We have what we've been seeking, what has been seeking us, and in receiving that we know that LOVE is all there is. We couldn't lose it if we tried!

Establishing a relationship with the Mentor is turning to Unconditional Love. We find where it can always be experienced, inside ourselves, and we learn to receive it. As that relationship deepens, our need to receive it from "outside" diminishes, as does the fear that we will lose it from a person "out there." If communication with your partner goes south, and the voices start a fear-mongering conversation about how you're going to lose his love, you can pick up the recorder and talk to the Mentor. You're back in relationship with a LOVE you cannot lose.

Now communications don't have to be fraught with fear. Communications don't have to mean anything more than an exchange of information. Talking with your partner is just talking with your partner; you don't need to be fooled into thinking this is an exchange that means you do or do not love one another. In fact, being in an intimate relationship is a wonderful opportunity to practice including "another" in the Unconditional Love we find in ourselves.

Gasshō,

ch

Meeting Our Own Needs

Dear Cheri,

Are you saying that an R/L practice is a way to show up for myself in a way someone else cannot? I get to meet my own

needs rather than relying on someone else? I am excited about that prospect because no matter how effectively I communicate, no matter how hard my partner tries to be there for me, it seems the reflection I'm looking for rarely happens.
Sincerely,
Curious

Dear Curious,
     Beautifully stated. **We** know what we need. What a coup for ego voices to convince us that what we need needs to come from someone else for it to be meaningful. If we've been paying attention, we know we've never been able to provide for another person what they want and need. We might come close at times, but it's never 100%. We give loved ones a break because we know they're trying, and, if we're lucky, they will do the same for us.

But what we're seeking will never come from "outside." WE meet our needs, and then we're freed up to be as unconditionally loving as we can be with others.

From that clarity, we can be open to and appreciative of the efforts at Unconditional Love others are making. It's not Hollywood, but it is the only thing that truly satisfies.
Gasshō,
Ch

We All Belong

Dear Cheri,

I changed schools every other year growing up. It was hard to make friends, to face the gauntlet of strangers with regularity and find a way to fit in. It was not my experience that people were kind. That feeling of being the "new kid" is with me in all social situations now. I'm tongue-tied, awkward, afraid to mingle, afraid to put myself out there and connect with people. I want friends but it feels easier and safer to be reclusive and say nothing.
Sincerely,
Always the New Kid

Dear Always the New Kid,

It may feel familiar to be reclusive, but it's definitely not safer. When you are "by yourself" you're actually not alone. You're in constant "relationship" with the voices in your head, listening to stories that reinforce the identity of the "new kid," friendless, awkward, afraid, no social skills. You'll never experience anything different in a social situation unless you're allowed to step out of that story. This is where R/L can be of tremendous assistance.

With the Two-Handed R/L Exercise, you can begin to hear from the new kid. You can listen to and connect with him. You'll learn to be truly present to his experience, present with the one who had the experience rather than believing the ego/self-hate stories you are told in conditioned mind. As the relationship grows, you'll have clarity about the difference between that child back then and the adult who is ready to take a rightful place in the world now.

There's no hurry here! The most important work is finding compassion for all

concerned. Compassion happens naturally with presence.
Gasshō,
ch

Being a Social Relief

Dear Cheri,

I often feel relief when I communicate my hurt feelings to my partner. Are you saying that's not a good idea, that I should use the recorder instead?
Sincerely,
Puzzled

Dear Puzzled,

It's certainly something to investigate!

Ego uses the word "communicate" and we're meant to follow it off to "communicate" ego's "hurt feelings" to someone. Or we could say, "Blame and point out what someone did wrong." But I'm communicating, the voices whine. Same word, very different process. Rather than let ego voices drag an innocent person into what ego is trying to do, pick up the recorder for a heart-to-heart with the Mentor. With practice, you'll quickly be able to recognize ego's manipulative shenanigans. You'll hear what *you* need to address to take care of yourself, and you'll recognize what the voices are doing to sow seeds of discord. *All ego wants is attention.* Getting you (all of us) to complain is a great way to get attention. Perhaps that's why complaining is so popular!

Gasshō,

ch

Who Are We Saving Really?

Dear Cheri,

I usually don't say anything when someone hurts me. I just deny or repress or ignore it. Recently, I was able to share that what was said was hurtful. The person I was with was offended! Should I not be able to say what is so for me?

Sincerely,

What Happened?

Dear What Happened?

Denying, repressing, and ignoring happens when we listen to voices telling us not to say anything. This doesn't take care of us. However, blurting whatever pops up to say might not be the best thing to do either.

It's often most helpful if we talk with the Mentor about our hurts and grievances using Two-Handed recording. It can be distressing to finally get up the courage to say something to a loved one only to have them get hurt and upset over what we said. That kind of reaction will be taken up by ego to become a "just keep your mouth shut" message.

Most hurts turn out to be insightful places in our growth. They don't need to involve anyone else. It's also helpful to remember that we have no control over another's reactions. Ego would have us believe that every negative reaction is our fault. "If you had been _____, everything would have been fine." "If you had said _____, everything would have been fine." That's simply not true. There are folks for whom anything other than unbridled approbation is an occasion for offense.

Getting clear about what is true and real and important for us opens a path to choose if and when we want to engage with another person. Often, it's just not worth it. Our own clarity is what matters to those of us practicing awareness. What other people say and think is really none of our business.

Gasshō,

ch

Getting Support

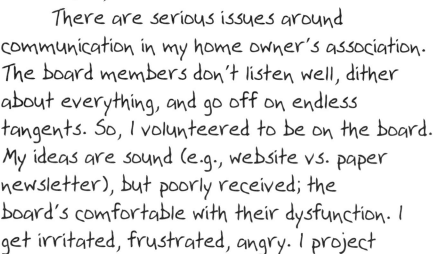

Dear Cheri,

There are serious issues around communication in my home owner's association. The board members don't listen well, dither about everything, and go off on endless tangents. So, I volunteered to be on the board. My ideas are sound (e.g., website vs. paper newsletter), but poorly received; the board's comfortable with their dysfunction. I get irritated, frustrated, angry. I project unkind things about their intelligence and competence. I want to pick up my marbles and go home.

I don't want to act out from this upset and I'm ashamed that I get so upset. How would you suggest I practice with this?
Sincerely,
Frustrated

Dear Frustrated,
        This is a perfect occasion for a Two-Handed Recording Exercise. Here's how it can work: You and the Mentor begin a practice of taking on the home owner's association as a vehicle for your enlightenment. You talk over everything about the situation. You get to rant and rave (recorder in the right hand), listen to that person's agony (recorder is in the left hand), and then receive the Mentor's wisdom and compassion (recorder still in the left hand). You go to the meeting or send in the suggestion or whatever is next, and the two of you talk over what happens with you. Every bit of what egocentric karmic conditioning/self-hate does to you will be revealed through this practice. And your loved ones don't have to suffer through it with you! This is one of my favorite aspects of R/L—we no longer have to subject others to

every nuance of the relationship with egocentric karmic conditioning/self-hate we're in the process of ending.
Gasshō,
ch

Healing Old Wounds

Dear Cheri,

My brother and I are estranged. He reached out to me because he is sick and possibly dying. I want to be there for him but I'm afraid that as we begin to communicate, all the anger and betrayal and hurt that I have harbored against him will spill into the conversation. I don't want what happened in the past to take away from the possibility of the connection we're attempting to have in the present. I'm also worried about his health but I don't think he wants to hear about my worry.
Sincerely,
Tentative

Dear Tentative,

This is another good spot for some Two-Handed R/L.

Pick up the recorder and let that person who harbors anger, hurt, and betrayal talk about that experience. Let it all pour out. In the privacy of your own recordings you don't need to be afraid to feel and to *express* all that you feel. When you've said it all, let the Mentor respond to that person. This is an intimate exchange between you and the Mentor that frees up YOU, the authentic human being, to interact with your brother. If you don't take care of the hurt and anger, the odds are huge that egocentric karmic conditioning/self-hate will attempt to ooze in and poison this new relationship. Handling with the Mentor all that goes on with you in communication means you don't need to be afraid of what the ego scrambler will try to do in your interactions with your brother. Do that same R/L practice to process the feelings of worry you have for him.

Gasshō,

ch

Having Our Feelings

Dear Cheri,

I had a couple of experiences where other people were upset with me and I listened. When I listened, I realized that their "upset" had nothing to do with me and were simply things they were processing. And I still feel disappointed that they got upset. What would you suggest?

Sincerely,
Disappointed

Dear Disappointed,

Yes. Someone is upset; you don't need to take that on or take it personally. When we don't make what someone else is going through be about us, we can be a compassionate presence to hear them. You can just listen, nod understandingly, make sympathetic noises, and get on with your life. Does not taking on what someone else is going through mean you're unfeeling, that you don't care? No. It means that you realize you don't need to let ego grab the spotlight and try to be the star of someone else's show. Keeping attention off of conditioned mind and on the other person is how we realize we *do* care about others.

If "someone" has disappointments about relationships, you can pick up the recorder, hold it in your right hand and let that person express. Put the recorder in the left hand, listen to that recording, hear that person, listen for the Mentor's wisdom and compassion, and get on with your life.
You're here,
   you're aware,
      you're seeing everything that's happening.
      You're watching Life unfold, and you're not letting ego hijack attention to use any of it to cause you to suffer. This is very good, isn't it?
Gassho,
ch

Choosing What Is True
Dear Cheri,
   I'm feeling challenged around business conversations and sales calls. I'm always afraid that I'll embarrass myself and the

company. When I make a call, I am already nervous, defensive, and off balance. And more often than not, I say or do something unskillful. I'm looking to be more relaxed about these interactions. I'm highly qualified. Why can't I be confident, at ease, and relaxed?
Sincerely,
Feeling Unsuccessful

Dear Feeling Unsuccessful,
    The voices talk you into being nervous, predicting bad, embarrassing outcomes, and then they tell you that you shouldn't feel the way they've made you feel! It's the same set of voices on both sides of the net. "You're going to mess it up" comes the first serve. "You're messing it up" is the return. "You shouldn't be messing it up" comes from the other side. "Why can't you be confident, at ease, and relaxed?" is

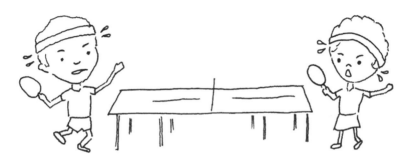

the follow up. Back and forth it goes. No wonder we get off balance.

As you may be suspecting by now, the best way I've found to get past those voices is Recording and Listening. We have to replace that suffering-causing conversation in conditioned mind with what's true. What's true is that you're highly qualified. You do a great job. You'd be a perfect choice for anyone looking for the kinds of services you provide. You're capable, responsible, professional, reliable, and operate in integrity. I don't know this but I'm betting it's true and you can fill in the details I missed.

When we record we don't flatter. We're not doing affirmations. We just say what's true, what's so. That's plenty. And, since it's true, the voices can't accuse us of lying or wishful thinking. Just start making those recordings and listening to them often. The voices will come up with all kinds of "you don't sound sincere, you have an awful voice," and other useless crapola designed to stop you. Just keep going. Record. Listen. Gain insights. Record those insights. Listen. Imagine you as the coach of your dreams and begin to coach the "you" who is being undermined by nasty ego voices.

In the process of internalizing the messages from a coach who loves you unconditionally and wants the best for you, an interim step is to listen to your "this is what's true" recording right before you make a sales call or participate in a business meeting. And if you're still hearing hateful voices during a call, have one earbud in playing your recordings while you're making the call. Just let it be softly reassuring you about what's real. In time, what is true will more likely be what you're hearing— even without recordings—than what the voices want you to believe.

Gasshō,

ch

Talk about the Good Stuff

Dear Cheri,

I pick up the recorder and talk about what's going on with me. When I do that, I realize I no longer feel the need to tell the person I have communication

issues with everything I told my recorder. So, what do my partner and I talk about now?
Sincerely,
Interested

Dear Interested,
You get to talk about whatever you choose! You get to talk about what is so for you in the moment, in the present, right now. Your question assists us all to see how thoroughly we're conditioned to believe that if we're not focused on conditioned mind and its faux problems, we'll fall into a giant void of

My sister is feeling a lot better. She...

My breakfast was delicious. I had...

RECORD IT ALL!!

I love walking in the park.

Work went well today. We...

My cat did the cutest thing!

I like my new neighbor. He's...

nothingness with nothing to say, nothing to do, nothing to be interested in or care about. Talk about ego nonsense! The entire universe is available to us when we cease directing attention to ego.

Fun practice to consider: Notice how you go through most of the day with, primarily, neutral to good stuff going on. Most things work: car starts, phone has service, no one gets sick, has to go to the hospital or dies. In fact, with a little scrutiny you realize some really good stuff happens every day. There are kindnesses, successes, little triumphs, happy moments. But when you get home and someone asks how the day was, conditioned mind leaps to the fore to report on that one "bad" thing that happened. It's a habit to let ego do that. The practice alternative?

Start noticing every good thing
that happens all day long.

Beautiful weather, smiling faces, little wins, something you enjoyed eating, a pleasant phone call.... As we start paying attention—and tracking those—we realize we have lots to talk about with loved ones when we get home.
Gasshō,
ch

Changing the Conversation

Dear Cheri,

    Are you saying that R/L assists me to communicate better with other people because it changes the way I talk to myself?

Sincerely,

An R/L practitioner

Dear R/L practitioner,

  That's exactly the case. Improving "internal" communication will improve all communicating.

We are trained to believe
we can live in an internal conversation
that is critical, judgmental,
hateful, and punishing
while having kind "outward" conversations.
We cannot.

    We must be present to what's going on with us, see and hear what's going on inside our head, or be doomed to suffer, acting out externally what goes on internally.

    That suffering is not just in the realm of communication. This process of R/L we're practicing will wholly change how we communicate with other people, true; however, the first, best result will be a wholly changed life for ourselves. When we're no longer giving attention to the nasty nonsense ego drones on about inside a conditioned head (and, yes, we've all been conditioned), we're free to be present, enjoying Life as Life is rather than remaining trapped in a tiny, claustrophobic, fake reality of ego's making.

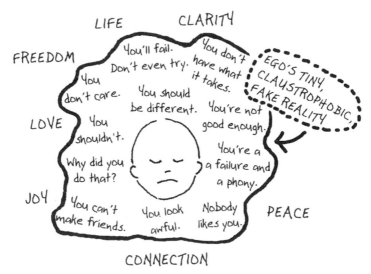

Final point: You mention "the way I talk to myself." This is not "you" talking to "yourself." That's the big scam we need to see through. That's a karmically conditioned ego conversation, more akin to a recorded program than anything current that's "playing" inside your head. If you watch and listen closely, you'll be able to catch on to the fact that you are NOT talking. You're *listening* to what's being said and you're being bamboozled into believing you're doing the talking. That's one of the "top three" most important awarenesses to have in Awareness Practice, so put it at the top of your "will focus here" list, please.

Gasshō,

ch

Will focus here
1. Watch for the "I'm talking" bamboozle
2. R/L all of it
3. Pay attention

Compassionate Communication Is...

People talk all the time, but that's not the same as communicating. As we said at the beginning of the book, "good" communication happens only when ego is absent. When the ego voices are operating, words are happening, but what we hope to accomplish through communication is not.

To *communicate* is to be able to *see* what is *so* and to *say* what is *so*. It implies being present to what *is*, which means attention cannot be on a conversation in conditioned mind. In practice, we often use the phrase "dropped in" to describe how information comes to us. It's not "I think," it's that "it just came to me." The difference, while dramatic, is difficult to catch. The difficulty lies in not being accustomed to looking **where** it's occurring.

The "drop in" of being *informed* by the Intelligence that's animating us has a new, fresh feel to it. We often have the sense that, "Huh, I would never have thought of that." On the other hand, the "occur" that happens in conditioned mind feels familiar. There's a "yep, that's me; that's how I see things" quality to it. If we're *present* as the information arrives, we see clearly where it came from. The first simply *appears*; the second is *presented*.

Not giving attention to conditioned mind opens the possibility of another aspect of communication: the ability to *listen* and to *hear*.

When we're able to listen to and hear
someone without interference from ego voices,
and we're able to see what is so
and say what is so for us,
we have the possibility
of actually communicating.

It is helpful to stop and take in the magnitude of that. Without the ability to keep attention on presence, it's not possible to listen to and hear another person; it's not possible to articulate what drops in for us as clear, compassionate and appropriate to say. If we cannot drop the interference from conditioned mind and bring attention back to thisherenow, we're giving voice to ego, but *we're not actually communicating.*

Realizing this can put us immediately in touch with what we conditioned human beings are up against. No wonder we struggle. No wonder we feel misunderstood, frustrated, hurt, and confused. We've been trying to do something we have been *trained* not to be able to do. And, to add insult to injury, we've been punished by self-hating voices for being unsuccessful.

Let's take a moment to allow in some 1) compassion for all of us and 2) appreciation for our heroic efforts to keep playing against a stacked deck.

FACILITATION: Three Techniques

The term we use to describe communicating from presence is facilitation. To facilitate is to practice engaging with another human being without allowing ego to sabotage, hijack, or distort the exchange. It's not an easy task, and far easier than ego has bamboozled us into believing.

In addition to being the only way to truly communicate, facilitation practice has at least three other benefits.

1) It's a great kindness to ourselves.
2) It's a great kindness to others.
3) It's probably the best training we can have for learning to direct attention away from the conversation in conditioned mind.

Facilitation uses several techniques for being present in interactions. We will look at three of them:

1. **Reflecting**
    2. **Clarifying**
        3. **Drawing Out**

1. Reflecting

What usually happens to us when someone else is talking?

Attention wanders to...
a judgmental thought, dismissal of the person's experience, rehearsal of our response, impatience to provide the answer or solution to the problem, eagerness to share a more extreme example of the content, desire to express an opinion, and more!

As attention wanders, the ego scrambler leaps into operation, and the centered human is nowhere to be found. The ego reacts in its self-centered, ineffectual ways and authentic communication is missed.

Here is the way an ego communication could go between two people sharing a house:

Linda: Why can't you ever take the garbage out when it's your turn! Why do I always have to remind you? Why do we have to talk about it each time?

Rose: That's not fair. I do take it out. I don't know why you think I won't and feel the need to constantly remind me!

Linda: If I don't remind you, it goes out late. Then we have a full garbage can and there is nowhere to put the garbage that piles up during the week. I hate not being able to take trash out during the week. You know that. You just don't care. (To herself: I get so sick of her. She's so self-absorbed.)

Rose: If you care so much, take it out yourself. (To herself: I really need to live alone!)

We can see the ego scrambler in operation here. The voices are talking through Ego Linda and Ego Rose.

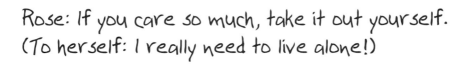

The alternative is a technique called Reflecting. To reflect is to mirror back what someone says as accurately as possible. It's not to summarize or paraphrase; it's not to interpret; it's to repeat back their words as closely as we are able. It requires the attention to be HERE, attending to what an actual human being is saying rather than what ego's voices are droning on about inside the head. When we reflect back what the other person said rather than going with what the ego voices are saying, we have an interaction in which ego is excluded.

If Rose were reflecting, the conversation might go this way:

Linda: Why can't you ever take the garbage out when it's your turn! Why do I always have to remind you? Why do we have to talk about it each time?

Rose: What I hear you saying is that you would like me to take the garbage out when it's my turn without having to remind me or having a conversation about it each time.

Linda: Yes. It would make my life easier.

Rose: It would make your life easier. I can see that.

Reflection avoids letting ego grab hold of the conversation. Linda can say what she feels. Rose's reflection allows Linda to have her experience while giving Linda the opportunity to get clear about what's going on for her by having what she's saying reflected back to her. It allows Linda to feel heard, validated, and understood.

If she reflects, Rose doesn't have to make it about her. She doesn't have to explain, defend, justify, or maintain a position. In reflecting, Rose is not required to agree with what Linda is saying. Reflecting enables Rose to allow Linda's experience to be true for Linda, even *if it is not true for Rose.*

Anyone hear a voice asking,

 Yeah, but is she going to take the garbage out on time?

That's ego wanting to grab the attention and make a problem. We don't know that this first exchange will resolve Rose and Linda's issues, but if they continue to communicate in this kind, open, respectful way, their odds of getting to a place of mutual agreement go way up.

The power of Reflecting is that it's no longer about the garbage. Whether Linda is right or Rose is right is not allowed to interfere with an authentic connection between them in which each gets to have her own experience and is heard.

It might take several iterations of this discussion to resolve the issue of when the garbage goes out,

but the magic is in
two people working through an issue together
rather than putting a problem
between them and fighting over it.

Sometimes people, in the grip of an ego-identity, get upset if their exact words are repeated back to them. The voices in the head hate and resist Reflecting because it takes attention away from ego and places attention where it belongs—in the present. That's okay. Just keep in mind that a person who is resisting being heard is not present. That person is identified with ego, and it may take some negotiating before they get free enough from ego to be open to in-the-present communication.

It's possible to use the "spirit" of Reflecting as we become more practiced with the skills—and our loved ones become more amenable! With practice, Reflecting can become quite sophisticated.

For example, Linda says, "How many times do I have to remind you to take out the garbage!"

This could result in violence rather than communication if Rose replied with, "I hear you saying, how many times do I have to remind you to take out the garbage!"

But if Rose said, "Uh-oh, it sounds like you're letting me know the garbage did not go out yet!"

It's still Reflecting. It's still keeping ego at bay.

Here are some other examples of the spirit of Reflecting:

Your friend says, "I don't know why you keep going to that restaurant; the food is awful." Regardless of your experience you might reflect with something like, "So, you've had experiences of their food being awful?"

Perhaps your father-in-law states, "Putting some money aside every month is something you're going to be grateful for in later years." Whether you agree or not, you can respond with a reflection along the lines of, "It sounds like putting some money aside every month has worked well for you."

The Benefits of Reflecting

Reflecting gives us the opportunity to take a step back from the kneejerk ego impulse to give our opinion. We can listen, hear, and take in what someone is saying *without taking it on or taking it personally.*

The greatest gift we can give is attention. Listening, hearing, and reflecting allows someone to feel heard.

One of the surprising results of Reflecting is that when we are speaking we often don't know what we just said! Reflection allows us to hear ourselves!

2. Clarifying

We are so conditioned to reference the conversation in conditioned mind that we don't realize how often we assume we know what someone else is saying. Clarifying is the technique of asking a person to explain in their own words what they mean rather than our going up into conditioned mind for "clarity." This requires us to be present to know that we don't know and are getting ready to assume.

For example, perhaps you say to me, "I don't feel like working." What? Is that global? Now and forever? Some particular work? Rather than leaping in with whatever conditioned mind might be projecting at the time, I can find out by asking you some clarifying questions such as:

You don't feel like working right now?
Do you mean you don't feel like working ever?
Is there some particular work you don't feel like doing?
Are you saying you don't want to go to work?

Let the person answer, and then reflect what they say. If you realize you're still not certain what they're saying, ask another question. Continue asking until both of you, with a little help from the next technique (Drawing Out), are clear about what's being said and heard.

Linda shouts, "How many times do I have to remind you to take out the garbage!" Rose could ask a clarifying question such as, "Do you feel that you always have to remind me?"

An exasperated Linda might retort with a sharp "Yes!" (Here, she might hear the "always/ never" nature of her question/accusation.)

If Rose is present, she might follow up with, "Hmm, that hasn't been my experience, but I don't want you to have to remind me so

I'll pay attention to that. Would you still be okay reminding me if I have a lapse?"

At this point Linda would likely have difficulty keeping wind in those sails that Rose's openness is emptying. Once again, we have two people on the same side resolving a shared issue.

3. Drawing Out

Because most of us are conditioned to listen to voices that censor what we say, we're not given to offering complete information. Drawing Out is the technique of assisting someone to say what they mean. As with Clarifying, Drawing Out is a way to show interest in the other person and to signal willingness to hear all they have to say.

How to use Drawing Out

Rose: I had a really horrible day at work.

Linda: I am so sorry to hear that. Say more?

Here, Linda opens the door for Rose to elaborate. Rose feels heard and has the opportunity to tell her friend about her day.

If Linda says "No kidding; I had a miserable day as well," the conversation is liable to stop right there, leaving Rose with no chance to say what is so for her.

After Linda facilitates Rose's experience, Rose can return the favor with something like, "Do you feel like telling me about your day?"

There are Drawing Out phrases such as "tell me more" and "then what happened?" and "can you say more about that?" but sometimes just sympathetic, understanding noises, along with a sympathetic, understanding facial expression, are enough to encourage someone to say more.

Assist Someone to Disidentify

Dear Cheri,

I have communication challenges with a subordinate. I ask questions to gain clarity. They get flustered and seem not to know. I interrogate. They change the subject. I'm frustrated because this person is not doing the job they're hired to do. They should know the answers. I get impatient and push harder, but the harder I push the less I get out of them. It's exhausting and ineffective. I feel bad about how I deal with this situation. I'm sure my employee is suffering as well! How can I deal with this situation differently?
Sincerely,
Exhausted

Dear Exhausted,

When we identify with the voices of egocentric karmic conditioning/self-hate, we treat others the way the voices treat us. As you point out, it's exhausting and it doesn't work. Time for a different approach. Instead of demanding information, you can assist the person to give you what you need. You can *facilitate* a process that enables them to get to the clarity *they* need to give you the information *you* need. For instance, rather than interrogating, Reflect what they say. When they don't seem to know, ask (gently, if possible) if there's something they're not clear about.

Draw them out of their anxiety by assisting them to get out of the conversation with the voices in their head and instead in to a conversation with a nonthreatening you.

This is the essence
of facilitation.

Gasshō,
ch

Be Interested

Dear Cheri,

    Tonight I met with an old friend who talks too much and suffered mightily during a twenty-minute monologue. I didn't want to hurt him by cutting him off. I didn't want to create any awkwardness between us by interrupting and telling him that he was talking too much. And I so wanted just to leave. I felt resentful at being trapped in this situation and conflicted because I actually do like him.

Sincerely,

A good friend

Dear Good Friend,

    You have here an excellent opportunity to facilitate.

    A facilitator often has to break into a monologue with something like, "Hang on a second; I want to make sure I'm following you." Once the interruption is achieved, it's possible to Reflect what the person has been saying. Often the person delivering such a soliloquy as you describe isn't listening! Having what they're saying reflected back to them creates a marvelous opening for mutual exchange and keeps the facilitator from drifting off into boredom and judgment. Being there with attentive awareness is a true gift to give to another. Plus, it's a way to participate in a conversation rather than being kept out of the conversation by a voice in the head telling you that you are the victim of a bore!

Gasshō,

ch

Not Taking it Personally

Dear Cheri,

When my intimate partner is angry, he often lashes out. I want to say something but I can't think of anything to say. Instead I withdraw. I feel hurt by what he says. I'm ashamed I can't stand up for myself. I resent the fact that he gets to give vent to his anger and I just have to take it. But I don't say anything and the cycle repeats. It feels hopeless.

Sincerely,

Muzzled

Dear Muzzled,

Well, there's a lot going on here, isn't there?

There's a big clue in your description that "when he's angry, he often lashes out" and you "want to say something but can't think of anything to say." This tells us that the anger is his and has nothing to do with you. If it did have something to do with you, there'd be something you want to say back. You might still be afraid to say it, but you'd know what it is. You would know what "your side of the argument" is. Instead, you withdraw and hear a conversation in your head repeating what he's said and feel hurt.

This is another big clue: You feel "hurt." "Hurt feelings" are ego's bailiwick. He's angry and lashing out. Why should you be hurt about that? There's no reason, of course, but you feel hurt because ego voices in your head are telling you what he's saying is true or it's not true or that's how he really feels, etc. Nonsense. He's upset and spewing. End of story.

What happens next? The voices start in on you about what's wrong with you that you don't stand up for yourself. *They shame you for the fear they create in you!* That's so important to see. The self-hating voices are shaming you for being afraid. Where is that fear coming from? From listening to and believing what the voices are saying to you! The voices create the fear and then shame you for feeling it. Outrageous, yes?

What happens next? The voices start a rant about how wrong it is that he gets to do that (vent his anger) and that you just have to take it. Hogwash. He's venting. "Taking it on" is your choice. Which is where R/L is going to make the difference for you. You can still withdraw, only now it will be with your recording device to process with the Mentor what's going on for you. Now you can vent! It's called Two-Handed Recording. You can say everything you feel but have never been allowed to say out loud, and you can get support to realize that what he's doing has nothing to do with you. All your difficulties with "him" are, in fact, difficulties with ego voices in your own head.

Then when you're feeling ready—keeping in the front of conscious awareness that all of life is a giant Awareness Practice workshop—you can try this: As your partner starts to wind up, you can hold up a hand and say something like...

"I get upset when you're angry with me, and I'm not able to hear you. I want to hear you! So, if it's okay with you, please stop every few minutes so I can reflect what you're saying and be sure I'm hearing you correctly."

You haven't agreed to agree. You know his upset is his and his perspective is his. And, he's your partner and you love him and you want to find a way for both of you to be able to communicate such that your relationship can be loving rather than upsetting.

This may take a while. That's okay. You're learning, growing, changing, and, I'd bet, so is he. Gasshō,

ch

Staying Engaged

Dear Cheri,

I experimented with something in a conversation with a colleague. I did not contradict him, offer my opinion, or state my position. I did ask some questions. I felt he was way off base but I didn't say anything. The interaction felt really passive but it was calm. What does one do in an interaction where there is disagreement but the best course of action is not to engage or disagree without it flaring up into being an angry exchange that goes nowhere?

Sincerely,

Passively Listening

Dear Passively Listening,

Did you Reflect at all? If not, try that next time. Often people have no idea what they're saying. They're not listening to themselves. Their attention is on the conversation in their head and ego is doing the talking. When we reflect them, the other person has a chance to **hear what they're saying,** and maybe, just maybe, they might hear something they don't actually agree with! It's truly a gift if your reflection allows them to realize they're being ego's mouthpiece and they can perhaps come to presence as a result.

Will this always work? No. I've reflected people who have looked me right in the eye and said, "I didn't say that." Yeah, they did. Is it worth arguing over? Never. However, it is fascinating.

Paying attention,
being present to what's actually
going on instead of caught
in a conversation in the head,
makes everything fascinating.

Bringing awareness to your colleague, not just *what* he says (you may not be taking that in), but *how* he says it, his body language, facial expression, look in the eyes as well as bringing awareness to you in all the same ways (yes, we're talking about expanded awareness), you'll be so riveted you won't care about the content of what he's saying.

This is like playing a high-level tennis or video game. It takes everything we've got. If attention wanders for a second we miss an opportunity. We want to be HERE fully, nothing left over and nothing left out. Think of aikido. Two masters. In this way we don't think of the other person as an opponent. That person is someone assisting us to be the very best, and most present, we can be. This person is our teacher.

Nothing passive about this!

Gasshō,

ch

Whose Stuff Is Getting in the Way?

Dear Cheri,

I am challenged when I communicate with my mother.

Despite being forty years old, I move to being a child in relationship with an authority figure when she gets angry with me and criticizes me for something I've done! Lately, I've been trying to listen to her and see her point of

view. It's hard to do that without taking it all personally!
Sincerely,
Trying to listen

Dear Trying to listen,
Here is an unorthodox suggestion that you'll need to see for yourself about employing. Explain to your mother that when she gets angry and criticizes you, you can't hear what she's saying. Ask her if it would be okay with her for you to record what she's telling you so that you can listen to it later when you're not so upset. If she's in agreement, you'll have a much easier time working with the situation. If she doesn't agree, you could work with the Plan B that follows.

Plan B
Reflecting what she says aloud may not be a good idea—just yet. But you could reflect what she says silently to yourself. This would allow your attention not to focus on the voices that want you to get upset and withdraw. It would also assist you not to go to self-hate. In

this way, you can reflect just one set of voices (hers) berating you rather than taking on the internal voices attempting to pile on to make the situation worse.

As you practice this, a couple of things will likely happen. 1) You will be so busy facilitating inside your head that you'll move into an observer position with the whole thing. You won't be able to take in the *content* of what she's saying, and since she's telling you what you've done wrong that's probably a good thing. And, 2) if you can manage to nod, she might feel heard, which could end the tirade sooner.

In parallel, start working with the Mentor to see what goes on with you in these episodes. You become like a child. That's an important reaction to get to the other side of. You get upset. That's another one to see through. The Mentor will help you see that your mother's upset is her upset; it doesn't have anything to do with you.

"Angry and criticizing" is not the same as "having a point of view."

We must never lose sight of projection.
What other people say and do is "theirs."
What we say and do is "ours."
We don't do anything because of someone else.
Neither does anyone else.

(We must keep in mind that the fact that something is a projection doesn't necessarily mean it isn't true, but owning our projections is the key to our freedom.) Anyone can be upset with us. Anyone can wish how we are or what we do were different. Anyone can make a request that we alter a behavior they find troubling. We get to make the choices about how we are. We don't need to succumb to being controlled by anger and fear. If someone makes a request, we can choose how we respond.

    As your practice continues, you'll be able to hear what the issue is and you and the Mentor can talk about that as well. Perhaps, without all the anger and criticism, you'll be happy to go along with what a loved one sees as important.

Gasshō,

ch

Stay in Love

Dear Cheri,

I am challenged when I have to communicate with someone who espouses a perspective that is potentially harmful to other people, especially when they claim "higher motives." I get angry. I get upset. I react unskillfully. I lose the peace I want to feel. What do I say or do on these occasions?

Sincerely,
Not wanting to react

Dear Not wanting to react,

It's really hard. It's painful to watch people make choices that hurt others, and when we're not paying close attention that pain can turn us into people who would happily hurt them. It's quite fiendish, really. Staying in innocence, so that we can see and project innocence, might just be the most challenging aspect of spiritual practice. In this regard, spiritual practice is much more difficult than Awareness Practice. In spiritual practice, we're required to see "God" in everyone. Seeing "God" as them *and us!*

That's what makes facilitation such a great tool for situations like this. The techniques—Reflecting, Clarifying, Drawing Out—enable us to stay in the peace of wisdom, love, and compassion rather than getting pulled into ego's dualistic world of beliefs and assumptions. You care. I project you want to care about everyone and everything. We can stay with that caring only when attention is not pulled by ego into judgments and opinions that cause separation.

When we're practicing facilitation, so much concentration is required to listen closely and stay with a person that often we're not able to take in the content of what they're saying. There's no room for conditioned mind to leap in with its opinions about their opinions. If you practice Reflecting what they're saying, you can stay out of the identification that causes you to be reactive. You will get to stay with caring for the human being, sympathetic toward all of us who get identified with and act out of ego ignorance.

Gasshō,

ch

Curiosity Keeps Friends

Dear Cheri,

My friend commented that something I said was weird. I felt rejected and ready to defend myself. Then it occurred to me to just shrug and accept that as our interests diverged we would grow apart. If I can't say something and be accepted for what I say, why should we still be friends?

Sincerely,
Resigned

Dear Resigned,

Hold on a minute! We've got all kinds of tools to bring to the party that are way more fun than rejection, resignation, and losing friends. Your friend said your comment was weird. Okay. How about if the follow up is "Oh, really, how so?" This is what is called a Clarifying question and it brings us to that marvelous friend of clarity called "projection."

Your friend thinks something you said was weird. That's interesting. That doesn't have anything to do with you. It has everything to do with your friend. If you

ask the clarifying question, you have a chance to learn something about your friend.

The ego voice in your head "guiding" you wants to make everything about it. "You," identified with ego, take personally what your friend said, feel rejected, and then step away from friendship. Who's going to be your friend now? Yep, ego is right there to volunteer for the position. You can go home with it, sit on the couch, and listen to stories about what's wrong with you and everyone else!

Don't fall for it. You have all the tools you need to stay HERE, pay attention, receive insights, and step free of suffering. It's a way more fun way to live.

Gasshō,

ch

Dialogue versus Debate

Dear Cheri,

    My neighbor and I are on opposite sides of the political spectrum. We debate our positions and seldom agree. After these interactions, I feel exhausted and drained and wish I'd never taken the bait to debate him. I wish I could communicate my position to him and make him see how narrow his perspective is! If I don't say anything, it signals that I agree with him, which I don't. If I debate him, I'm sarcastic, cutting and judgmental, and all we are is further apart than we were. What kind of communication is possible in this situation?

Sincerely,

Searching for a way to dialogue

Dear Searching for a way to dialogue,

    The choice of words here is interesting. You and your neighbor *debate*. The word debate has a connotation of arguing for a position. On the other hand, the word *dialogue* has a sense of talking together to reach an understanding. The first is not likely to result in the second. When ego is involved, the outcome is seldom agreement. We could define ego as a position, in fact, an op-position. Because the ego's sole interest is in maintaining itself, all debates serve only to shore up its position.

It might be important to understand what you're looking for in these interactions with your neighbor. Is your neighbor interested in your perspective? Are you interested in his? Are these interactions meant to be a way to connect? If so, you could certainly engage with him on a topic and really listen to what he says. You could reflect what he says. Reflection doesn't mean you agree, but it is a way not to let ego into the exchange. You could practice some Drawing Out and Clarifying techniques along the lines of, "So, are you saying that…?" Then reflect the answer. Follow that with, "What I hear you saying is…. Is that what you believe?" You'll become so fascinated by the process that you'll have nothing left over to get hooked by ego's attempts to drag you into opinion and indignation.

There's another technique that might be fun to introduce into your dialogue. When you reflect follow it with "Yes, that's interesting, and...." which is where you insert a perspective. Hear what the other person has to say, Reflect until you feel clear, and introduce the "Hmm, yes, I see, and...." See if you can keep yourself to one clear, simple point. "Hmm, yes, that's interesting, and if we don't learn to care about one another, what do we have that matters?" "Hmm, yes, I see, and I'm still going to go with loving my neighbors."

Here's another one of those unorthodox suggestions: Put a recorder in your pocket and record your conversations "for training purposes," as they tell us in the world of customer service. No one else will ever hear them, but you can use them to get clearer about your process.

And never forget the importance of keeping a sense of humor.

Gasshō,

ch

Don't Be Distracted, Clarify

Dear Cheri,

    I'm a nervous interviewee. When I'm asked a question I don't understand, I feel paralyzed. I'm aware of thinking, "They're going to think I'm dumb, that I don't get it. I need this job. I can't screw up...." And because I'm thinking about that, I miss what is said. Now I can't answer the next question and have to ask the interviewer to repeat it. It's really the most stressful process!

Sincerely,

A bad interviewee

Dear bad interviewee,

    You lay out the process so clearly! Someone asks a question. Attention goes to the conversation in your head. "They're going to think I'm dumb, that I don't get it. I need this job. I can't screw up..." You're distracted by those voices and aren't present. Now you miss what's being said. The voices then continue with their beatings.

If you were not believing the conversation in your head, you would know what was being asked of you. You'd hear it. If "not understanding" didn't get interpreted as "there's something wrong with me," you could simply ask for more information—you could use your facilitation skills! You heard what was said. You could follow up with a reference to the language in the question and ask a clarifying question of your own, "Are you asking if I have skills in....?" If you're present, if you're paying attention, if you're listening, the person interviewing you will know that.

You don't have to be a mind reader. People who don't have your particular internal voices might assume they know what they're being asked and be completely off.

We have a virtual program called Reflective Listening Buddies (RLB) that allows a person to practice Reflecting. In the program, you learn to be present and reflect as your Buddy talks for 15 minutes. While you're practicing that, you get to watch the voices work hard to do to you what they're doing to you in those interviews.

Distract. Attack. Criticize. Doing any and everything to throw you off. You're meant to get confused, feel bad, feel stupid, and, of course, want to quit. That's always the bottom line with ego—quit doing whatever you're doing that threatens its absolute control. But with RLB you get to practice reflecting whatever you heard, and asking your Buddy to repeat what they said, in the event you got distracted. And then you talk for 15 minutes and your Buddy reflects you.

Gasshō,

ch

Be the Change

Dear Cheri,

In my last couple of encounters with my family, I have been practicing asking for what I need and expressing myself clearly. It did not go well! I was surprised at the reaction I received. I thought I was being clear, but my clarity was not appreciated!

Sincerely,

Surprised

Dear Surprised,

Folks who are used to us being a particular way will often react with defensiveness when we "change the rules." "This is new, not sure what's happening here, am I safe? Is our relationship changing? Does this mean s/he doesn't love me anymore?" That can seem preposterous to us, but we have to remember we live with what's going on in our head, no one else is privy to that. Inside the other person's head is something like, "You're being different. I don't know you. What does this mean?"

Not taking it personally allows us to stay with people rather than letting ego jump in to take a situation from bad to worse. This is your family. This means years of "you're that way and I'm this way and this is how we are," right? Now you want to change that. That's threatening to everyone's ego.

This is where those facilitation skills come in handy. You can Reflect, ask Clarifying questions, and Draw Out until everyone feels good about the exchange. There might be things about the family dynamics that other folks

would like to be different. You can find out what those are. With practice, over time you can gently, with lovingkindness and compassion, assist the family to a new way of being together. It only takes one person to make these changes. The challenge won't be as much in your relationship with your family as in your relationship with ego. Ego will be the big loser as you trade your relationship with it for a new relationship with your family.
Gasshō,
ch

Being Heard

Dear Cheri,

I have realized that if I breathe, relax and really listen to my partner, we don't end up arguing so much! It does mean that I don't get to talk a lot but listening seems to work.
Sincerely,
Enjoying listening

Dear Enjoying Listening,

It's funny, isn't it, to consider how much of "communication," according to ego programming is "I talk, someone else listens, hears me, and agrees."

Listening? We can *listen*? We can listen and reflect and move toward *understanding*? What a notion, huh? Even more miraculous, sometimes when we really listen and move to understanding, another person seems to want to do the same thing.

Facilitation skills might be something both of you learn to enjoy. As with Reflective Listening Buddies, you could do it "formally," with each having a specific time, or you could just develop the habit in daily exchanges. And it *is* a habit. First it's a habit of presence, of awareness, and then it's a habit of being fully *with* another human being. It's truly loving and, in fact, has saved many a relationship.

Gasshō,

ch

Processing

Processing is another effective communication technique. In fact, it may be as effective a path to true communion with another human being as is facilitation.

The mechanics for processing are simple.
-- I say what's going on for me.
-- You then say what you see for you in response to what I say.
-- I then respond with what I see in what you say.
-- And so on, back and forth

There is only one ground rule:
Each person completely owns their experience. What do we mean by "owning one's experience"? Let's say you had a disagreement with your partner and you'd like to talk to them about it. If ego were talking, it might say: "You hurt my feelings when you went ahead and made a decision without first consulting me. We had an agreement and you broke it."

If you own your experience, you might say... "It upsets me when I'm not consulted over something we made an agreement to collaborate on." Subtle but different.

The objective when processing is not to settle anything on the level of content. We don't solve a problem, resolve a conflict, arrive at a compromise, come to an agreement, or win an argument for one's position. Processing is a protocol to exchange information. It's a safe way to be vulnerable. It allows me to get clarity about what's going on for me and for you to witness that. If you choose to, you can facilitate me.

If we're processing about a situation that involves you and me, then we each get to talk about what goes on for us in the situation. The situation/the problem/the decision is not the subject of the exchange. *Our process*, how we are in the situation, what we feel about it, how we can be with it is what's being explored.

Let's say we're housemates and fight constantly over dirty dishes in the sink. A conditioned conversation may go along the lines of:

A: Why can't you ever do the dishes?

B: That's not fair. I often do the dishes. I just don't do them when you think they should be done.

If we were processing...

A: Can I process something with you?

B: Yes

A: I'm aware that I get upset when there are dirty dishes in the sink. It's not really about the dishes! It's just that I'm exhausted at the end of the day and coming home to a pile of dishes feels like the last straw. I snap because I don't have the energy for one more task. It feels like I'm the one for whom a clean sink is important and I get upset when it seems as if what's important to me is not being considered.

B. I don't mean to be defensive when you point out the dishes have not been done. I'm just disappointed that you think I don't do my fair share of the work around the house.

When you start a conversation with the words, "I'd like to process something" you're conveying that you want to engage in a specific form of communication. You're setting up a structure where you would like to talk about what goes on with *you*, and you would appreciate  the other person's attention. Like an old-fashioned telephone exchange that used to "put through a call," a connection to exchange information is being put in place. The person receiving this opening gambit understands your intention and indicates their willingness to engage with you in this protocol.

Processing, at its best, is true communication because it bypasses the ego. Here's how:

-- When I'm looking to see what's going on for me, I'm exploring my experience of ego identification. I'm looking **at** it rather than **through** it. Rather than acting out of it, I'm disidentifying from it.

-- When I'm not identified with ego, I'm present, at center, more available to see and connect with you.

-- When we're processing together, *you* are also bypassing ego and more available to **me**.

　　We're both focused on what we share rather than what separates us. We're in the process of connecting. We're communicating.

Some Techniques to Try

-- Ask for External Input

　　Summoning the courage to ask for input from sources *outside* one's head can result in illuminating information. I've received the same input *inside* my head for so long I simply assume it's true. I sound arrogant or condescending or whiney or needy or like a know-it-all. Really? We're afraid to ask because we're told what we're going to hear will be devastating. For this reason, we want to choose judiciously whom to ask. Start with a close friend and consider how you want to phrase the question. For instance, I might say, " I'm told, inside my own head, not by anyone else, that I talk in a _____ way. Is that your experience?"

172

If we remember that we're bringing conscious awareness to what have been sources of suffering, we will be well-prepared for the response. Perhaps your friend looks at you in astonishment. "What? No!" and you feel a "whew" of relief. But maybe your friend says, "Well, sometimes you sound sort of _____, but it's not bad." Or, perhaps your friend says, "No, I think sometimes you sound _____, but not _____" Can you get a sense that you could survive this? That it's interesting? That you're getting some information that has the potential of freeing you from the tyranny of the judging voices in the head? (And, of course, we must never lose sight of the fact that our friend, much as s/he loves us, **is** projecting.)

Once we catch on to the benefits of looking to sources of information outside conditioned mind, we can begin to bring conscious compassionate awareness to all aspects of our communication.

Two points to keep in mind:
1) The only person who can be an authority on how you are is you. Not a partner, a parent, a

child, not even a best friend—you. With Awareness Practice we're learning to have direct experience and gain clarity through insight. When we're HERE we receive all the information we need to move from suffering to freedom.

2) When your friends tell you their experience of you, trust them over hateful voices in the head. Your friends like you. The self-hating voice in the head most emphatically does not.

Might you benefit from some refining? Of course. We all can benefit from refining, but the changes we're going for happen in love. In practice we say, " I love you exactly as you are and I will help you be any way you want to be." That's what we're going for.

-- Use a Preliminary Phrase
Most communication struggles come from the fact that, since childhood, we have been in an intimate, often unnoticed, one-sided relationship with negative, punishing voices inside our head. The messages we hear might not literally be the same as those we heard from

adults when we were children, but they *sound like* what we heard. The result is that even though I'm now an adult, when I consider saying something an adult might not like, I feel the fear that I learned to feel in childhood, and I emotionally become that frightened child.

It can be helpful to learn "the power of the preliminary" for these occasions. A preliminary phrase serves two purposes: It can defuse an anticipated negative reaction from the person we're talking to, and it can serve as a calming, centering technique in potentially frightening circumstances.

"I don't know if this will be helpful, but..."
"You may have thought of this already, but..."
"This is just something that occurred to me..."

I can use one of these intros the way one might take a long, steady breath before launching off a diving board. It can prepare me for whatever might come next. If what I get back is unfavorable, I'm in a much better position to receive it because I've let myself know this is a scary proposition, and I've already indicated I'm not here to threaten anybody.

It's good to remember that folks close to us read us as readily as we read them. You've watched me come in from work often enough to be able to sense whether now is a good time to talk about a problem with the kids or if that might be best left for another time. And if we don't really know (since our reading of the situation is a projection), we can communicate!

We could say, "There's something I'd like to talk with you about. Is now a good time?"

Moreover, if we have our communication skills at the ready, *and we really want to communicate*, it doesn't matter how the other person responds or reacts. "NO! Now is NOT a good time," comes a snarling answer. "I've had the world's crappiest day at work, I'm in a filthy mood, and I don't need any more problems." (Kind of want to duck for cover?) Another possibility is something along the lines of, "I'm so sorry. What happened? Want to tell me about it?"

Without the voices in my head going off in unhelpful directions, I can be HERE for someone having a hard time. I might get a blow-by-blow of the world's crappiest day at work, I might get an "I don't want to talk about it," or something somewhere in between. It doesn't matter. I'm doing Awareness Practice, and, being present, I will see a lot, however this goes. I will see what arises in conditioned mind. I will practice coming to presence and staying present. I will use my facilitation skills. When it's all over, I will make and listen to a recording of all I've seen and learned. I cannot lose.

Practicing Compassionate Communication

The many
Rs
in Communication

If we're not present, communication is nothing more than a conditioned **Reaction** followed by a **Review**.

Example: Ellen has a hard time saying no. She's conditioned to believe that the right person thing to do is to accommodate every request. If Bob asks Ellen to do something for him, the conditioned **Reaction** from Ellen would be to say yes. She's likely entertaining a conversation in her head that goes something like this:

-- I should say yes.
-- Should I say yes?
-- I can't say yes. I have so much work to do; I can't take something else on.
-- But I can't say no. It's Bob! Bob wouldn't ask me for help if he didn't need it.
-- What kind of friend are you? How can you refuse to help him?

-- He would be so hurt if I said I couldn't help him. He'd never understand.
-- Well, I suppose I could work on the weekends if I need more time.

Ellen says yes. And right on the heels of that yes is the **Review**. The voices in her head will criticize her with messages such as "Look at you. You can never stand up for yourself! You are such a doormat. How could you agree to that? You don't have time!"

We can circumvent **React & Review** with the following techniques:

Reflect: In Reflecting, we listen to what someone says and then repeat it back to them as closely as we can. Since we cannot have attention on conditioned mind and be present at the same time, **R**eflecting allows us to bypass conditioning. It gives us time to be **r**esponsive rather than **r**eactive.

Record: Picking up the recorder is the best way to direct attention away from conditioned mind and get HERE. With **R**ecording and Listening we can **r**ehearse what we might want to say as we go into an interaction. With Two-Handed Recordings we can process what happened in an interaction in which we got identified with ego and **r**eacted. We can find compassion for falling—again—into an ego bamboozle. We can clarify what's going on for us. We can talk through our anger, disappointment, hurt, betrayal, and fear with the Mentor, and from that place of compassion for ourselves we can arrive at the information we want to exchange with another person.

Respond: This takes mastery! **R**esponding requires us to be present enough to be clear about what to say and to say it from presence. This takes constant practice. We don't practice this skill only in difficult situations; we practice it in every exchange we have.

In our example with Ellen and Bob, Ellen could say, "Can you tell me more about this?" (clarifying if this is really that important to him.) "I have a lot going on. I want to do this if my assistance will make a difference." When Bob has offered more information, Ellen might say, "Let me look at it and get back to you." Communication is a practice.

We're experimenting. We're looking to see. We're curious. We're not assuming. We're endeavoring NOT to look to conditioned mind for information. We're practicing looking AT conditioned mind, not THROUGH conditioned mind...

...and we are developing the ability to speak from a disidentified perspective.

A Zen Guide to Compassionate Communication: How to Practice

First, we must realize that ego identities are carrying on a conversation in conditioned mind, and that we mistakenly believe that's "me thinking."

Next, we get clear that we're committed to the practice of freeing ourselves from the system we call egocentric karmic conditioning/self-hate. That commitment gives us the courage to proceed.

Then, in every situation we practice watching and listening to what the voices say, noticing how that conversation makes us feel and how it controls us.

Through Recording and Listening we get in touch with what's going on for us.

With encouragement from the Mentor, we grow comfortable with experimenting,

gaining confidence that we'll be fine
no matter how any interaction might go.
We choose a situation to practice facilitation,
rehearse with the Mentor, and jump in.

We don't entertain reviews. No post mortems.
We don't refer to conditioned mind for an
evaluation.

We prove to ourselves that any information we
need will drop in through insight.

We R/L about what we saw so that we don't
lose our insights.

We choose our next situation....

As we practice in this way we can expect the ego voices to scream in resistance. This is how we know we're on the right track.

I keep you safe!
I'm the voice of reason!
I'm your common sense!
You don't have a chance
without me!
I've protected and guided
you all your life!
You're nothing without me!
You won't survive!
Everyone will
take advantage of you!
You're a fool!

Let's explore how to work with our most challenging communications.

Work on What You Have to Resolve First

Knowing what sets us off is important,
if we don't want to suffer
when we interact with others.

As we pay attention to the conversation inside our head, we begin to realize that we don't react to what we are not conditioned to be sensitive to! I have no investment in my handwriting so make fun of it all day and I'll laugh along with you. Joke about my old beater and I'll help you because my identity isn't in the kind of car I drive. But raise even an eyebrow when it comes to how I handle an area of responsibility and you've just picked a fight.

This is the kind of thing that's impossible to prove, but certainly raises our suspicions: We seem to attract the very people who push the buttons we're most sensitive to having pushed. As we get clearer about our hot buttons, clearer that not everyone is set off by what sets us off, we can begin to observe this phenomenon. Am I more attracted to people who will poke at my sore spots? Is the upset I feel so familiar, in a comfortably uncomfortable way, that I unconsciously *choose* people who will trigger me? Am I simply replicating my childhood? Does it feel safer to stay in my world of "knowing" how people are and how I'll react than to enter a world of unknowns? If my primary ego identity is wrapped up in being a victim or misunderstood or not belonging or never meeting the standards, what will happen to me if I'm around people who don't reinforce that identity?

It's also helpful to understand our own motives. If I want something to be different— how I feel, how you behave—I can know I'm operating from an ego identification that is likely designed for disaster. I'm in a conversation in my head trying to figure out how not to feel the way I feel. If I could be different or, better yet, if *you* would be different, I wouldn't have to feel the way I feel.

It's important to understand
that none of this is aimed
at feeling better.

The framing of the problem, the desired
outcome, and the approach all share the
purpose of maximizing suffering.
It's good to know what we truly want, and
to know the ego-identity we're willing to
surrender to have what we want. Perhaps the
most difficult point for us to see is that what
ego wants and what the authentic human being
wants might *sound* the same but are vastly
different. The ego and the human being may
both express wanting love. However, while the
human being longs for Unconditional Love, the
ego is going for suffering. The ego is Hallmark
cards and movies, romance novels, and, yes,
pornography. The ego offers impossible
scenarios that promise satisfaction and deliver
suffering. Authenticity will happily let go all of
ego's "desires" in order to feel the love that is
unconditional. As we continue to pay attention,
this difference becomes stark.

Recording and Listening practice gives us a kind, wise, mentoring presence with whom to discuss what we're bringing attention to, *which is infinitely more compassionate than being in a hateful conversation with ego in conditioned mind.*

Dear Cheri,
I am often unkind in my communications. I can't help it. I say something mean or sarcastic. I can watch how this affects people around me but I sometimes just can't help myself. I would like to be kind. How can I do that?
Sincerely,
Trying not to be mean

Dear Trying not to be mean,

Actually, you can help it. Identified with ego, you're letting self-hate do your talking. Remember, self-hate and other-hate are the same thing. You, at center, are not unkind. Or self-hating. All that mean, sarcastic, self-hating stuff is what happens when you go unconscious, when you're not present and ego takes over.

We can have kind communication with folks *outside* the head only if we're having kind communication with ourselves *inside* the head. When we're consciously paying attention, we see that inside and outside are the same. Of course, we can fake kindness with others, which we've long been encouraged to do, but it doesn't actually work. We're ending suffering here, not trying to fool people (and deities) to get a good report card. As we practice to end punishing conversations inside the head, we're equipping ourselves to choose kind communication with those "outside" the head.

Make some recordings that reflect the kind world you want to live in and from.
Gasshō,
ch

Dear Cheri,
What I find frustrating in
communicating is the response I
receive. I want to connect. I want to have fun.
So, I make a joke or say something funny or ask
a question to elicit a connection. It's often not
well received. I feel rejected because no one
wants to play with me!
Sincerely,
Want to Play

Dear Want to Play,
        Let me ask you this: Is playing appropriate
in those moments? Is that what's going on? Is
that where others are focused? Have they
agreed to play? If not, and an energy of "I just
want to play with everyone" comes
in uninvited, it can feel intrusive rather than
fun.
        And that's the set up. "I" wants to play.
Attention on "I want to play" stops you from
being present to the situation, sensitive to
whether play is appropriate or not. When "I
want to play" runs into the energy of what's
going on with other folks, "I" interprets that as

rejection reinforcing the story of disliked, resentful, frustrated, misunderstood, and picked on or whatever ego's story is.

After you've looked at that, how about if you start seeking playmates in play situations? An improv class? A sports team? A service project like cleaning up a beach? Group hiking or bike riding? It will still be necessary to be sensitive to what you're sensing about people's mood, but your chances of finding people in a lighthearted, open-to-having-fun mood will be better.

Final point: As you bring conscious awareness to this issue, keep an eye on unconsciously seeking situations in which the conditioning will be reinforced.

Gasshō,

ch

Dear Cheri,

I try to be supportive of my partner. I'm always there when she needs something. I pretty much agree with doing what she wants to do most of the time. But communication breaks down when I ask for some time alone. She gets hurt and upset. I do care deeply about her but I feel disconnected from myself after spending a lot of time with her and I feel completely justified in taking some time to be with me. It's not that I don't want to be with her. It's just that I don't want to be with her all the time!

Sincerely,

Agreeable

Dear Agreeable,

When you're with your partner, being agreeable, are you aware of a conversation in your head about what you should say, how you should be, what you should do, etc.? Is it possible that what you don't want to be in is *that* relationship? You don't want to be in relationship with the voices in your head all the time? That's an exhausting relationship to be in!

Which doesn't mean you wouldn't want and shouldn't have some time with just yourself. That said, I would ask you to pay attention to when the conversation turns to "wanting some me time." Is it when you start to become aware that you actually like spending time with

this other person, that you're *present* when you're together, that you're actually enjoying yourself? Ego is a jealous "lover." It wants you all to itself and doesn't like competition. Look to see whether you're being lured into some "quality alone time" with ego or whether you're truly seeking a way to be more present, more centered, more HERE.
Gasshō,
ch

Dear Cheri,
    I have received feedback that I have a really strong personality — that I'm loud, overbearing, aggressive, argumentative. I can't seem to communicate without offending. People always seem to feel hurt or wronged when I interact with them. I always end up feeling there is something wrong with me. So nowadays, I try not to say anything.
Sincerely,
Something Wrong with Me

Dear Something Wrong with Me,

Well, of course, I'm the last person to agree that there's something wrong with you.

I hear you have a conditioned belief that your personality is "too," followed by a "negative." What if how you are emotionally were seen as passionate, vibrant, heartfelt, enthusiastic, and spirited? Would there be a problem? No. But how "you" are has been painted in a negative light. That's the conversation in your head you're trained to listen to and believe. Since that has long been established, how you react to how you are (also conditioned) is a problem.

How about if we go back and examine the original premise? What if there's nothing wrong with "your" energy? If there's an issue at all, what if your energy is "too" perfect, "too" just right, "too" just how Life wants you to be? If we accept that, which for the record I would suggest is true, then what might the real problem be?

A place to look: Perhaps it's that others are feeling left out of your excitement.

Perhaps rather than including others, you, in your enthusiasm, tend to forget about them, talk **at** them rather than **with** them? Overbearing, aggressive, and argumentative will probably always play better in a boxing ring than in polite society, but that doesn't mean your heartfelt passion can't be presented in a way that others find energizing and supportive. Talk it over with the Mentor and come up with some small experiments to implement.

Gasshō,

ch

Dear Cheri,

I can't express myself honestly and authentically with my partner. I tell myself, "Don't rock the boat, you always make him the bad guy. What you want/think isn't important." At some point, I explode at him over something. Now my internal monologue is along the lines of, "You've done it now, you have to fix it. You never say or do the right thing!" Some of my attempts at reconciliation are met with resistance or

withdrawal because my partner is not receptive to talking about feelings and behaviors. I feel disrespected, isolated, misunderstood and project he doesn't care.
Sincerely,
Can't Communicate

Dear Can't Communicate,

Well, he IS your partner, right? If he really disliked you as much as the ego voices in your head would have you believe, he'd likely be gone, wouldn't he? It's true there are people who stay in a relationship *because* they can abuse, but let's just look at your part in this.

What you've expressed here is threefold: He's wrong, you're wrong, and it's wrong. He's the way he is and that's not good enough. You're the way you are and that's not good enough. The situation is the way it is and that's not good enough. The only winner here is ego!

What if none of what those voices are saying is true? What if there's nothing wrong? What if this is just a big workshop to assist you to learn to choose Unconditional Love? You know that's true, right? **But we get talked**

into living as if it isn't. We forget that giving attention to negative voices in the head is the bottom line of how we're made to suffer.

What to do? How about taking on
being what you want from him?
How about treating both of you
the way you want to be treated?

No one has to know you're doing this because it will all happen in your R/L practice with the Mentor. You'll be living out the prayer of St. Francis, seeking to love rather than to be loved, to console rather than be consoled, to understand rather than be understood.

That practice, "doing what you want to have," will change your life and, who knows, we hope it will change your partner's as well.
Gasshō,
ch

Dear Cheri,
I am reeling from an encounter with my father. He told me in his

usual highhanded and critical way to deal with something. I was hurt and I lashed out at him. This has been our "communication pattern" forever! I have practiced with just breathing in these encounters since I know I can't change how he is, but I guess I was caught off-guard. Am feeling terrible.

Sincerely,

Reeling

Dear Reeling,

That ego-maintaining complex of conditioning and self-hate often lulls us into unconsciousness. It fools us into thinking the "next time" will be different.

What you've realized is that "how he is" is a problem only when you're lulled into unconsciousness, fooled into believing that he isn't going to be the way he is. You can see that, yes?

What if he wanted you to be different? "When is she going to stop asking me to do stuff that's hers to do?" Over and over tries to "signal" you that he's not open to these requests. But you keep asking. Why d you do that? You do it *when you're not present.* You're right, we have to get in and learn to stay in our breathing mode (present and conscious) *because when we're not in our breathing mode ego **will hurt us.***

Think of him not as your critical father but as your own Bodhisattva, there to assist you to remember to be present. It'll help. A recording reminding you of this will be even more helpful.

Gasshō,

ch

P.S. Ego will often whine at this juncture, "Why do I (pretending to be you) have to be the one to do all the work? Why doesn't he have to stay in his breathing mode?"

The answer is that
you're the one who wants to
wake up and end suffering.

Talk to the Mentor First

As we have said previously, we are conditioned to believe that repeating what the voices are saying to someone else is "communication." It's isn't. It usually produces the exact opposite of the connection that communication hopes to achieve. This is why our best encouragement is to be in a relationship with someone—the Mentor is an ideal choice—with whom we can process what is going on for us before we talk to someone else.

So, stop often, breathe, make some recordings about what you're seeing, listen to them, and plunge ahead.

Dear Cheri,
I'm afraid to be honest with people about what's going on for me. Most of the time, my attempts to share

devolve into an argument. How can I practice
expressing myself?
Sincerely,
Afraid to be Honest

Dear Afraid to be Honest,
    The voices in our head are the first and
biggest stumbling block when dealing with other
people. *Those voices are framing our whole
world all the time and we usually have no idea.
You might hear that "he really didn't like what
you said" or "she never wants to listen to you,"
when the only evidence you have of that is that
you're being told it inside your head.*

The good news is that
we no longer need to be "honest with people"
because we have a tool
for being honest with ourselves.

The trap we've fallen into
is that I want you to understand me,
listen to me, hear me—
even though I haven't done that for myself.

As we continue to pay attention, as our relationship with the Mentor gets clearer through R/L, we realize how much of what we've been conditioned to believe about ourselves isn't true at all. What I've believed was "honestly me" is a story that keeps ego in control of my life.

The place to practice expressing yourself is in a Two-Handed Recording. Here's a refresher: Express everything. Say it all. Don't hold anything back. Then play it back and really hear what that person is saying. Be the listener you've always wanted to have. It'll take time, but before long you'll realize you don't need to "be honest" with other people because all your issues are resolved. You'll be with people because you enjoy being with people.

Gasshō,

ch

Dear Cheri,
    Professionally, I facilitate people communicating what they want in difficult situations. In contrast, I'm

challenged when I'm called to communicate something I want in a difficult situation. I usually don't want to bother others. If the communication is "not that important" I avoid communicating. If the communication is "important," I do speak up but I back-peddle or minimize my needs/complaints. I fear rejection but end up feeling rejected anyway since I don't make my needs clear.
Sincerely,
Accustomed to Rejection

Dear Accustomed to Rejection,
　　In other words, when it's not "you" involved there's no problem with conversing in difficult situations, no problem with speaking about what someone wants, yes? So, it's not the situation or the difficult or the wanting, it's that it's "you." At work would you ever encourage someone in a difficult situation not to bother others, not to speak up for themselves, or to back-pedal and minimize? No. Therefore, we can conclude that this is simply about leaving you out. That's the essential piece to see.

Here's what I want you to look into: You fear rejection from others, but the only place you're actually *experiencing* rejection is inside your own head. I'm so convinced that's what you're going to discover that I'm going to give you the antidote:

Start an R/L practice aimed at expressing clearly and kindly in a straightforward manner what you want. Watch what happens when you consider saying that to someone else. If you actually have a plan to deliver your message, you'll hear what the voices say in their attempt to stop you. Now, we both know those voices are not trying to stop you in order to take care of you, right? They want to stop you because as you get the hang of doing this—and you *are* a professional, after all—ego will lose a big weapon it's been using to control you.

When you feel clear about what you want to say and how you want to say it, say it to whomever you've been stopped from communicating with. Do this as an Awareness Practice workshop! Watch closely what's happening inside your head *as you* express

yourself. You'll see it's ego's fear that has been stopping you, not yours.
Gasshō,
ch

Is that so? Is It true? Questioning the Voices

Ego voices are able to do what they do because we're deeply conditioned to believe them. But if we train ourselves to question what they say, we can move out of ego's tyranny and into present moment experience.

Dear Cheri,
I hear the words I need to say in my head but watch and do nothing. By the time I respond, the matter has been settled. I build up anger about things but can't express it.

Sincerely,
Deer in the Headlights

Dear Deer in the Headlights,
    It might be hard to imagine just now, but you're in an excellent place in the practice of conscious awareness. Can you see that you could not have written that first sentence if you weren't present and aware? (This is where I point out that "you," the authentic human being, are the awareness that is aware of all that is happening.) You "hear" what you need to say as you "watch" the situation unfold. What's stopping you from responding? Attention turned to conditioned mind where there is enough noodling about should you/shouldn't you that the moment passes, to be followed by a self-hating message, something like "what's the matter with you, why didn't you say something?"
    Watch how that happens and I bet you'll see the critical juncture is when attention goes to conditioned mind rather than simply saying what you've seen and heard to say. Admittedly, this is a scary option *because* that's where ego defends its territory. People are cowed with,

"You need to think about what to say. If you don't, you'll say something stupid. You'll be wrong, get in trouble, people will hate you." All the things we were traumatized with growing up still control us.

It might be helpful to consider that matters are rarely irrevocably "settled." Rather than letting anger build you can practice, at the first hint of the voices in the head stoking the anger, re-visiting the subject with the other player with an, "After further consideration...."

Gasshō,

ch

Dear Cheri,
    I notice a lot of fear arises
which prevents me from asking. What I'm afraid of is that someone will say no.

Sincerely,
Afraid

Dear Afraid,

Yes, the voices will talk us into being afraid of finding out for ourselves what happens when we receive a negative response. What's the worst that could happen? I project that you've had that experience. True? It's never as bad as the voices threaten it will be. And really, what we find we cannot stand is what the voices do to us after we ask, which is simply another tactic to ensure we never risk asking for what we want. This is how the ego stays in control of a life.

In the situation you present the voices are talking you into being afraid to find out what happens when you get a "no." But as you continue to watch you'll realize the voices try to get us to be afraid to find out what happens—everywhere, all the time, in every situation, not just with "no."

In Awareness Practice we're finding out. Our questioning is along the lines of "Is that so?" "Really?" "Huh. Well, let's see." Living in fear is no way to live. As we explore, waking up to what's so in the process, we realize living in

fear is not living at all. In fear, ego is living our life as we tremble anxiously on the sidelines.
Gasshō,
ch

Dear Cheri

I'm not able to discuss past hurts or injuries with friends or family members so the issues fester. When I'm nice or act as though everything is okay with these people I feel fake and lose respect for myself. When I've been honest about my feelings in the past I've been misjudged so I keep quiet.
Sincerely,
Can Never Win

Dear Can Never Win,

You're making a *choice* not to get into stuff with certain people in your family because you *choose* not to deal with the fallout. Your experience tells you that saying what's going on with you is not going to result in anything you want, right? Does making that choice mean you're "fake"? Of course it doesn't. You're acting in accordance with a conscious choice. Are you nice? Sure. Why wouldn't you be? You've decided you're going to behave as if everything is just hunky dory with these folks—*because you don't want to deal with egocentric karmic conditioning's self-hating drama!* Now, your job is to shut down the voices in your head that want this to be a problem, want to replay old hurts and injuries, want the anger to fester and grow, and want you to feel upset about having made—and keeping—a mature, Awareness Practice choice.

Fortunately, we no longer have our previous choices of 1) keep getting into old stuff with family or 2) stay quiet and suffer. We now have Recording and Listening and the wise, compassionate counsel of the Mentor. We can talk it all out, feel heard, and continue to choose the grown-up responses that conscious compassionate awareness brings us.

Gasshō,

ch

Dear Cheri,
    I have difficulty writing emails.
Resistance in the form of fear,
procrastination, confusion, and perfectionism
arises. Will I be able to say the right thing? I
don't know where to begin. Will people judge me
for what I've said and how I've said it? I feel
bad for feeling so stuck, for having this reaction
to something so simple.
Sincerely,
Feeling Bad

Dear Feeling Bad,
    The most important thing I want to
encourage you *not* to do is to feel bad. No
more beatings. Period. Done. Not happening.
Okay? You can do that. You can make that
choice. If you imagine someone verbally abusing
another person—or an animal—can you see
yourself saying, "No, that's not okay. You need
to stop that." What if it were a small child?
Would it ever be okay with you that that was
happening? Of course not. Might it be scary to
intervene? Yes. But you'd risk it because the
abuse is so cruel and unfair and just plain not

the thing anyone should be allowed to do to another.

In the same way,
you have the power to say no
to that internal abusive voice.

There's no email recipient out there judging and criticizing you. *The only place it's happening is inside your head.* Ego, the quintessential fear-monger, comes up with that stuff simply to control you and keep the attention on it. As you see that clearly, you'll start having real email exchanges with real people instead of those faux email exchanges with nasty voices in your head.
Gasshō,
ch

Dear Cheri,
    I have some really cool ideas that I want to present to my Home Owner's Association. However, I'm hearing those voices say that my ideas will be rejected. I feel like I need a counterstrategy to

rejection. Or should I just communicate what I
see and let go my attachment to their
reaction? I guess I could try to experiment with
offering my ideas no matter what they say?
Sincerely,
Afraid of Rejection

Dear Afraid of Rejection,
        Why not? The assumption being asserted
by egocentric karmic conditioning/self-hate is
that you will present your idea and if they
reject it, that's the end of the story. If Gandhi
had done that, India might still be under British
rule! Instead you can present your idea and if
it's rejected you can present your idea and if
it's rejected you can present your idea... You
can LET IT BE FUN! You can
become a broken record. You
just keep repeating what is
so for you. You can make
modifications. Their reactions might be valuable.
Could happen. You don't need to argue. You just
keep coming back with your perspective. The
idea may still be rejected, but at least
everyone will have heard it!

What if we...
What if we...
What if we...
What if we...
What if we...

216

The point here is that this is for you. You're practicing awareness. You're getting to see what ego does to you, how you're controlled by what it's saying to you inside your head. The voices claim our problems are "out there," "with them," but they're not. Suffering is, as they say, an inside job. Learn to engage with others from conscious compassionate awareness and problems dissolve. All of life becomes what it is—interesting, informative, illuminating, and fun.

Gasshō,

ch

Dear Cheri,
    I'm just not a good communicator. I usually feel inarticulate, inauthentic, and unclear when I express myself. I'm constantly aware of how stupid and uninteresting I sound to people. I do want to say what is in my heart to say but it never comes out the way I want it to.

Sincerely,

Not a good communicator

Dear Not a Good Communicator,

We will *never* be "good at" anything as long as we look to conditioned mind to assess our performance!

Not looking to the voices of self-hate for information is paramount. Yes, you really want to speak from the Heart, but that's never going to happen as long as all the attention is on the conversation in conditioned mind.

Here's the good news about your situation: You can see it all. Clearly. You know the expression, "A problem well stated is a problem half-solved"? Well, yours is closer to "solved."

Attention can be on only one thing at a time. Because attention moves from thing to thing faster than we can track, until we've had a lot of practice with awareness of expanded awareness, it can seem as though we're attending to multiple things at once. (Research has shown that multi-tasking is an illusion.)

In your case—and you are emphatically NOT alone in this—attention is on the conversation in your head rather than on the conversation you're having with another human being. You can't attend to both at once, and currently the internal conversation is dominant. As soon as you learn to withhold attention from conditioned mind, to keep it on what the other person is saying, and on what's dropping in for you to say, all those hateful judgments about how you are will cease to be believable.

Gasshō,

ch

Dear Cheri

I am challenged at communicating when strong emotion arises with my partner and also at work and with family. There is discomfort and fear: if people see how strongly I am feeling, it will make them uncomfortable. They won't understand or help me. When strong emotions arise, I withdraw (immediately and visibly), holding back until calmer and have the right words. Sometimes this is good and other times I just want to be able express my emotions to others, in the moment, especially my partner,

but am afraid of being overly dramatic,
irrational and difficult.
Sincerely,
Afraid of Strong Emotions

Dear Afraid of Strong Emotions,
    It's easy to see childhood conditioning in
our current beliefs and assumptions, isn't it?
"Overly" emotional children—which often
translates into any emotion I, the adult, don't
feel like dealing with right now, especially if that
emotion is one I was punished for as a child—
need to be controlled. We get LOTS of
information that "Emotions are unacceptable,
you need to calm down, and use your head."
That whole process happened to pretty much
everyone—with one degree of rejection and
punishment or another—and so when we
become adults, we react to ourselves and
others as we were
reacted to as children.
Just how it
is. However, that's not
how it has to be. All
you describe is happening inside your head.

DON'T CHECK
IT OUT! YOU
CAN'T ASK THAT!

BUBBLE

You're not saying to family or a partner, "I am living in an emotional straitjacket because I'm afraid if I express how I'm really feeling you'll reject me," are you?

How about checking out the reality of the story that's controlling you? It will be a great opportunity to practice with

1) not taking things personally,

2) catching on to what the voices in the head are saying,

3) using your facilitation skills (Reflecting, Drawing Out, and Clarifying),

4) processing what you're seeing with the Mentor via Recording and Listening, and

5) generally learning and growing.

Please keep in mind that even if others say, "I want you to be how you really are all the time," the voices of ego are going to reject that and continue to look for—and report on—negativity (nearly always fabricated) on the part of the other person. We have to get it that ego is the one holding suffering in place, not other people.

Gasshō,

ch

Dear Cheri,

I'm challenged when I have to communicate my preferences. Usually, saying what I need is weighed against the possibility of offending, being rejected, "taking up too much space." I believe that if I show up as I really am with my big energy, asking for what I need, having preferences, being spontaneous, I'll be rejected, abandoned.

Sincerely,
Afraid of Rejection

Dear Afraid of Rejection,

Here's what I'd like you to consider: If you are not being *you* in relationships, the people you're in relationship with are not relating to *you*. They're relating to someone else— someone you're pretending to be.

They aren't really rejecting you because they haven't had the chance to know you. But that's the result. You don't get to be in the relationship, and they're relating to someone nobody actually knows, someone who doesn't exist. So how about risking being you and finding out if people are horrified, repulsed, and running from you in droves?

Keep in mind that we're rarely asking for what we "need." We don't tend to get needs met by other people. You're contemplating asking for what you *want*. You're a grown-up, right? If you ask someone for something you want and they don't want to give you that, *you will survive!* If they don't like you that's fine; what's important is that you like you. Blessedly, most people respond well to authenticity.
Gasshō,
ch

Dear Cheri,

I realize that I am petrified of being put on the spot because of an expectation that I have to have the perfect response. If I don't, everyone will know what a phony I am in being the "expert" in my area and I don't want to risk that. So I try to avoid situations where I'm put on the spot.
Sincerely,
Not wanting to be put on the spot

Dear Not wanting to be put on the spot,

I wish every conditioned human (that would be all of us) could get it that messages to be afraid, don't trust people, they're going to hurt you, you have to be careful are in place only to convince us to "choose" to stay at home alone with egocentric karmic conditioning/self-hate!

Everybody hates a know-it-all. Everybody hates perfect people. We're conditioned to "have to be perfect" while simultaneously "hating anyone who is perfect." Great for ego; terrible for us. A PERFECT duality—from ego's perspective.

We're wise to realize that talking with *anybody* beats talking with the self-hating voices in the head.

Gasshō,

ch

Dear Cheri

I went to a meeting with the intention of staying as open as possible. Someone said something that I perceived as

critical. I watched myself shut down. I guess I don't have to stop communicating just because someone criticizes my presentation. Should I just be open to criticism? That doesn't feel fair to me.
Sincerely,
Wanting to be Open

Dear Wanting to be Open,
Our ability to stay in open-hearted, kind presence is going to give us so much more than ego's defensiveness ever could. Ego digs in with its "They're wrong," and the only winner in that scenario is ego. Someone is unhappy with you. That's okay. How can you help them get to a place of being happy—not with "you," just happily heard and accepted? That's all we really want, isn't it? I don't want you to feel bad; I just want you to hear that I didn't like what you did. Those are really different. "I don't like what you did" is a long way from "I don't like you," but ego can make them "one" in seconds. You hear what I'm saying, you sympathize with me, you make it clear that you want things to be different, and you've got a new best friend!

And, yes, those voices in the head will start in about "that's phony," but we're learning not to care what those voices say.
Gasshō,
ch

Dear Cheri,
    When my brother asked, "How are you," I replied honestly rather than serving up a platitude. There was dead silence. I wanted him to ask me about what I had said. I wanted him to inquire further. He switched the subject and we just kept talking. I was aware of being angry and resentful at the end of the call. What happened?
Sincerely,
Angry

Dear Angry,
    We can guess that since responding honestly is a challenging new behavior for you, it might have caught your brother by surprise? Perhaps he didn't know how to respond. Perhaps

he was listening to voices that didn't allow him to be present to you and your honest response.

Even though this is uncharted territory for both of you, ego is happy to point out that he *should have* behaved the way ego says he should. Does ego really care? No. But it's a great way maybe to get a little more suffering out of a situation already not going as ego would wish. What would ego wish? It would wish for you not to challenge it by being honest. If it could convince you that your brother is not responding in a way that works for "you," why bother being honest. Heads you lose. Tails you lose. And, not only is ego still in business, it's growing its business!

Gasshō,

ch

Dear Cheri,

Communicating with my husband is a challenge. He doesn't like being challenged. If I express my point of view, he says something cold and cutting and won't speak to me for days. If I don't say

something, then I feel resentful. So, it's catch twenty-two between self-expression and being punished. I fear losing love more than losing self-expression. So, I don't say anything. This feels really real to me!
Sincerely,
Bitter

Dear Bitter,
 There are so many programmed beliefs and assumptions here. "Expressing and challenging are synonyms." They're not. "Having someone "express" a cold and cutting opinion is a problem." It isn't. "Having your husband not speak to you for days is a problem." It isn't. "If you don't say anything you'll feel resentful." You don't have to.

The fear-producing, punishing,
loss-of-love conversation is in your head.
You don't have to give it
any attention whatsoever.

 Do you R/L? Truly, these issues can be cleared up in that practice. "Really real" is

perceived as really real because conditioning has framed it that way. Ego creates a problem and then tells you it's too scary for you to solve the problem. Can you see that? The voices tell you your choices are self-expression and loss of love, or don't express yourself, have love, and feel bitter. Those are not your only choices!
Gasshō,
ch

Dear Cheri,
    I find myself challenged when communicating with people I respect. I so want them to think well of me. But I'm constantly aware that as I speak, I'm scanning for any signs they're unhappy with me. And if I pick something up, anything at all, I tend to shut up, be abrupt, stutter, try to gloss over what I've said, restate it, justify, rationalize... It's embarrassing for me and I project for them!
Sincerely,
Embarrassed

Dear Embarrassed,

Yours is a clear picture of the *process* ego uses to manipulate us into suffering. That person is important to you so you need to become self-conscious to the point of paralysis, scrutinize them constantly for signs of rejection, and push yourself into solving a problem that doesn't exist. You can't enjoy the person you admire and respect and, very likely, before long they won't be able to enjoy "you" since "you" have been replaced by ego-self-conscious weirdness!

People can tell when we're focused on ourselves rather than them, and people can tell when we're focused on them rather than ourselves. The first is universally unappealing; the second is universally appealing. You so want the person you admire to think well of you that all your attention is focused on you with none left over for them! Time to get attention off of ego so you can give attention to what you admire and respect—which is not ego.

Gasshō,

ch

Learning to Ignore the Ego Conversation

We have to realize that *regardless of what the voices in the head claim,* the conversation in conditioned mind is *designed* to make us feel bad, to create and perpetuate suffering. I can be quiet, never make waves, never express an opinion, agree with others no matter how silly what they say is, and the voices will *still* beat me up for some sin or crime they say I committed. Perhaps, I'll get a beating for being a spineless wimp whose only concern is what other people think! We will *never* win with those voices. We will *never* be clear enough, smart enough, good enough or any other enough to please them. They're not please-able. Period. Our very best move is to ignore them.

Dear Cheri,
    How do I stop ego from interfering with being present?
Sincerely,
On a Mission

Dear On a Mission,
    If you were an alcoholic, how would you approach quitting? If you were starving, how would you approach finding the work that would pay for the food you need? These questions are aimed at getting you to consider that "noodling" is not the correct answer. If you're an alcoholic the only way to stop drinking is to stop drinking. The only way to get the work to get the pay to get the food is to get the work to get the pay to get the food! There's nothing else going on. If you quit drinking and keep attention on a conversation in conditioned mind about drinking, you kinda might as well be drinking—in the sense that your life will still be miserable. **We have to get to "Just stop it."** If we don't want all the attention on a conversation in conditioned mind about "ego-I-me," we have to 1) stop doing

that and 2) put attention somewhere else—
somewhere like HERE. Now. Present.
    Enroll the Mentor and the recorder on
your "THISHERENOW" mission.
Gasshō,
ch

Dear Cheri,
    I feel good when I've done a
good job communicating with my co-
workers. When I've been ineffective in my
communications, I feel bad. I tend to shut down
and not participate as much in meetings. How do
I make sure that my communications are always
effective so I don't feel bad?
Sincerely,
Trying

Dear Trying,
    Your wellbeing is *emphatically*
not dependent on the quality of your
communication with co-workers. Your wellbeing
is dependent on whether or not you engage in a
conversation with egocentric karmic

conditioning/self-hate inside your head. The proof is that, when engaging with that negative conversation, *you can be made utterly miserable when there's no other human being around.* This is critical: The only problems that exist anywhere exist between a human being's ears.

What you really have to shut down is the conversation in conditioned mind.
Gasshō,
ch

Dear Cheri
      There is a fear of speaking with my co-workers. There is a clinging to monitoring what I'm saying and a need to check in to ensure I didn't say anything wrong. There is an evaluation of me to determine if I'm a good person based on what I said. This makes all communication nerve wracking.
Sincerely,
Trying to be a good person

Dear Trying to be a good person,

You have articulated perfectly how that ego scam works, how ego remains in control of a human life. Now, having seen that so clearly, you can explore this: *Ego is* fear. Not that ego is afraid. It isn't. We feel the jolt of adrenalin at the "OMG" thought of "what if..." that we conditioned humans *call* fear, and we're trained to believe there's something wrong. Is there? No. But we're so brainwashed to believe those sensations *mean* there is that we have to practice **hard** to get past the fear of the fear. It's all done with the old smoke and mirrors, but we *believe* it's real and so we suffer.

The most difficult practice a student of awareness will ever take up is turning attention away from conditioned mind.

That practice is the death of the ego, and the ego fights dirty to save its imaginary "life." Here's something to consider: As you realize you're equal to your life—you can survive someone having an opinion of you that's less than 100% good—you'll begin to realize other people are adequate to their lives as well. In pursuit of that, you can say to people, "If there's anything you need from me, let me know" and practice waiting to hear if they need anything. If you've offended, they can let you know that too. Having a solid relationship with the Mentor will enable you to survive even that.

Gasshō,
ch

Dear Cheri,
    It's revolutionary to consider sharing my communication challenges with the people I find challenging to communicate with. Now I'm afraid of what they might do with the information. Would they use it against me? Would they disapprove of me?
    I experienced this when being interviewed for jury duty. When I confessed to not knowing the answers to the questions, I projected the questioner was annoyed with me.

Sincerely,
Afraid of being judged

Dear Afraid of being judged,
    Getting disapproval from ego will become a great source of fun as you continue to practice.
    What will "they" do with the information? "They" won't do anything with it that holds a candle to what ego has been doing to us with it! Conditioned people don't like "I don't know" as a response. The fact that it's as true for them as it is for us is not likely to impress them. That's okay. We each have to work out our own salvation diligently, and if having a happy heart is the "price I pay" for incurring ego's disapproval, I'm good with that! You?
Gasshō,
ch

Dear Cheri,
    I often can't say what I mean. There's so much second-guessing going on. It seems that as I say what I'm saying, there is a parallel track of what I could be saying, what I'm not saying, how I could say it differently or what I should not be saying.

I'm always left with the feeling that I did a poor job of passing on the information that I want to pass on.
Sincerely,
Second-Guessing

Dear Second-Guessing,
　　Having something parallel running through the head as we're speaking is pretty much guaranteed to be a recipe for disaster. Whatever is going on, I'm in trouble if attention is divided between "this" and a narrative I have to follow in my head. We can watch that happening with people all the time. They're talking along, their eyes go slightly unfocused and often slide off to the side, they forget what they were saying. Once you catch on to that process, it's obvious they're looking to conditioned mind, distracted by what's going on there.
　　It takes tremendous discipline and commitment NOT to let attention get pulled into conditioned mind. *Not being subjected to that second-guessing ego torture is worth any*

effort. Happily, learning to direct attention to thisherenow is fun and fulfilling.
Gasshō,
ch

Dear Cheri,
    I don't have a very good relationship with my sister. We don't communicate very well! She does something that annoys me and I immediately lash out. How do I break this deeply ingrained habit?
Sincerely,
A contrite sister

Dear contrite sister,
    Breaking habitual, deeply ingrained ego reaction is what we're all attempting. What you're up against—what we're all up against— puts us in a great position to see and see through *how* suffering is caused.
    As you start to pay closer attention, you'll see how the chain reaction unfolds. Your sister does something. Ego launches on its, "She's being that way, she does that, that's so wrong"

rant and you (identified with ego) are riveted by the "case" being made. "That's right," ego fumes, "it's completely unacceptable that she's that way!" And on it goes. Who's paying the price? You are. Is she suffering over it? Probably not. She's suffering over what ego is doing to her inside her head. It might occasionally be something along the lines of, "She is such a .... She needs to butt out and mind her own business," but we'll never know for sure.

The REAL habit you need to break
is listening to that conversation
inside your head.

And after you fall for ego's crapola again—and you will—don't entertain a single word of judgment of you from that same ego voice getting you to judge her!
Gasshō,
ch

Dear Cheri,

How do I know whether or not my communication landed? I scan for clues in the other person's face and tone of voice but I can never be sure they understood what I said or even heard it!

Sincerely,

Did it Land?

Dear Did it Land?

Interesting question. You could ask the person to reflect what they heard, making sure what you said was actually what was heard. The one place you don't want to look for interpretation is conditioned mind. Ego inserts itself in a pretense of attempting to figure it out, to know, to be sure. What if you never checked? What if you never "know"? Here's a radical notion: Rather than trusting ego voices to tell you what you want to know (always a disastrous plan), how about trusting that the Intelligence animating you will let you know if there's something you need to know?

Gasshō,

ch

Dear Cheri,
　　If someone I'm with gets identified and throws a tantrum or gets hysterical, how should I respond?
Sincerely,
Interested

Dear Interested,
　　We could "solve problems" for the rest of our lives OR we could realize all "problems" appear to exist only when we're not present. When we're HERE and someone "panics" or "throws a tantrum" or "gets embarrassed," it's not a problem. We don't need to have a *plan* for what to do. Plans and "what to dos" happen in the faux reality of egocentric karmic conditioning/self-hate. Get HERE and all will be revealed.
Gasshō,
ch

Dear Cheri,
　　I'm not in good health. I'm usually a good listener but when I feel poorly, I

242

find I don't have the capacity to listen. I don't want to listen to the fun things that people are doing that I don't have the energy to do. It's too painful. And I find I have little patience when people want to complain to me about their stressful lives. Because I feel bad that I cannot be more empathetic when I'm unwell, I just withdraw. Then I feel forgotten because no one reaches out to me. It's so tiring trying to be there for people when I'm unwell.
Sincerely,
Feeling Tired

Dear Feeling Tired,
     What ALWAYS makes us tired is the conversation in conditioned mind. During years of going in and out of profound depression, one thing I learned is that there's always enough energy for attending to what Life is offering.

If we only had an ounce of energy
in our body, ego would happily siphon it off
and try to make us feel bad
for not having more to give it.

As you look at what you've written, can you see the level of "communication" you're in with ego? How much you believe that what the ego is telling you is *your* experience rather than *its* experience? Job number one is to stop listening to what you're being told about how tired you are and how impatient you feel or how painful it is to listen to the fun people are having. When you do that, notice how much more energy you have. See if this gives you the energy to be more empathetic, to be present to what people are saying.

When you're not listening to that voice in the head, perhaps you can give voice to how you're feeling and what you need and invite someone to listen to you. And never forget that you have the quintessentially good listener and wise counselor in the Mentor.

Gasshō

ch

Practicing RESTRAINT

Remember, ego is the world of dualities. The voices are fond of yelling, "Don't say anything!" when communication would be appropriate, and they're just as likely to yell "Say something!" when what we'd be saying would be inappropriate. Acting out and lashing out would be the "communication" ego would encourage us toward, which is simply the other side of withdrawing, isolating, and resenting.

We're learning to be present.
In the present we will watch, listen,
reflect, clarify, speak, hear,
be open, and connect.

It's usually kindest to give ourselves some time and space to "be with" when we find we're in a charged situation. Something happens and there's a shot of adrenalin through the system, a big emotional reaction. That's a signal to pay attention, not a signal to "do something."

Dear Cheri,
   I can't be honest with people. I tell people what they want to hear. I go along with someone rather than disagree with them or state a different opinion. On the other hand, I'm free with my opinion of people when they're not around. I'm happy to say behind their backs what I could not say to someone directly. It feels dishonest when I don't speak my feelings, and worse when I gossip.
Sincerely,
Out of Integrity

Dear Out of Integrity,
   That's an ugly one, isn't it? If you're ready to face this head on and move as quickly as possible to free the human being from all that ego nastiness, here's a suggestion:
   When you find yourself "needing to lie" rather than state an opinion that might not be

well received, don't say anything. There are lots of ways to do this. You can nod, shrug, raise your eyebrows in an utterly non-committal fashion. If someone persists, you can mutter, "Gosh, that's a hard one" or "Well, I don't know" or whatever gets you out of the situation. I can promise you the voices of ego will be going ballistic with "But you're being dishonest!" and you can just enjoy the irony.

Next, perhaps even more challenging will be not to say a word to anyone else about the interaction. No bad-mouthing and no gossip. Ego's reaction to that will make the first hysteria look calm! What you'll be doing is taking away from ego every weapon it's been using against you. It will have no more ability to make you feel bad, and all of its attempts to do so will be crystal clear as you watch.

Gasshō,

ch

Dear Cheri,
    I love my father but I often don't agree with what he says. If I

say something, he yells at me and we both feel bad. If I don't say what I think, I feel awful that I'm not allowed to be myself with a person I love. How does an awareness of the conversation in my head help me in this situation?
Sincerely,
Conflicted

Dear Conflicted,
   Sometimes we find ourselves in a situation in which our choices are not ones we want.

If I say something, it'll start a fight.
If I don't say anything, I'll be a liar or a phony.

   We must remember we're *practicing awareness.* The great gift of practicing awareness is that it's possible not to let ego make the interactions be about a false "me."
   I'm here. I'm paying attention. I see what's going on. There, that's my part in this. Do I need to behave in conditioned ways that please that voice in my head in order not to be

called names? Of course not. What the conditioned voices in the head *project* onto me has nothing to do with me! *The process reveals ego, but it says nothing about me.*

So, what can we *do*? A person has expressed an opinion I really don't agree with. He's my father. I don't want to unleash a battle.

-- I can nod sagely as if I am deeply considering what's being said (which never hurts to do, by the way).
-- I can shrug and nod, signaling that this is a very large topic indeed (which it likely is).
-- I can look off pensively into the middle-distance muttering something along the lines of, "Hmm, I just don't know," or if that feels like it could launch another salvo, "That's big, isn't it?"

In every interaction we can choose ego, which is the experience of dissatisfaction, separation, hate, and resentment; or we can choose presence. Our code word for presence is Unconditional Love, and we choose

Unconditional Love for another human, not for an opinion. After all, you do love your father.

Also worth considering is that your father yelling at you isn't a big issue—unless you make it one. When he yells at you he feels bad. He loves you. He doesn't want to yell at you. If you don't take on his yelling, if you get it that he's just him being him, you both win. You get to say what you want to say, he gets to yell, and you can both practice not letting ego make the yelling mean anything.

Gasshō,

ch

Dear Cheri,

I have a Recording and Listening practice and I'm aware that I can take responsibility for the care of this human being, and that I also don't need to be dependent on another person for my care and well-being. I still have a heart-centered desire to be in a kind and supportive relationship with another human being where

honest communication is part of the
relationship. Isn't it possible to do that?
Sincerely,
Hopeful

Dear Hopeful,
   Anything is possible, especially with a
Recording and Listening practice. I project that
your relationship with the Mentor allows you to
experience the Unconditional Love that we're
all looking for. When we experience that kind of
Unconditional Acceptance, we're not looking to
be fulfilled by "the other."
   We can now explore what communication is
in a relationship. The "killer" word in what you
wrote is "honest." That's a word ego can really
get its teeth into. **The way to take the bite
out of ego is for each person to take
responsibility for their own needs.** When
that happens, communication is simply conveying
to one another what each of you is seeing in
your life. It's an exchange of information that is
not distorted in broadcast or reception
by the ego scrambler. You truly *relate*,
saying what you see is so for you and

SCRAMBLER
EGO

251

listening to what is so for your partner. (Facilitation skills *really* assist.) Hopefully your partner does the same. However, that's not a requirement. Your practice is not to take what the other person says personally. If you do, go back to the recorder to work it out.

"Honesty" is for and about one's self. First and foremost, our practice is to *be* the person with whom we want to be in an intimate relationship. (We have a book on relationship, *Be the Person You Want to Find*.) No ego wants that, therefore this kind of communication in relationship requires mastery. Practicing awareness gives us that mastery.
Gasshō,
ch

Dear Cheri,
  I can't bear silences. I watch myself jump to fill any void. I know this irritates my partner, but this is one of the ways I suffer most in communication.
Sincerely,
Afraid of Silence

Dear Afraid of Silence

You are not alone in this! Most conditioned people don't like silence. There are few places one can be with others where silence is possible. Even when honoring the passing of a respected personage, a moment of silence is difficult to achieve. There's fidgeting, coughing, shuffling of feet, and whispered conversation.

External silence reveals
the internal conversation,
which is dangerous for ego.
To avoid being seen, ego scrambles to distract.

The silence we're conditioned to fear is not the silence of another person, *though it certainly seems that way*. I'm in a meeting with the boss and the boss isn't saying anything. It's okay for a few seconds and then I start jumping out of my skin. "What's s/he thinking?" The voices in my head are going crazy. Finally I can't stand the discomfort and blurt out something I'm later told by ego was inane.

"*Talking just to fill the silence*" is often an unconscious habit. I don't realize I'm uncomfortable and I certainly don't realize the discomfort I'm feeling is coming from the conversation in my head. I feel nervous, anxious, and if I say something I'm distracted from the discomfort. Some of that nervous energy is dissipated in the act of speaking.

Staying still in the silence allows us to observe ego's controlling machinations. We cultivate this silence in meditation, in solitude and stillness, and it supports us in conversations with others. Trusting our growing ability to stay present, we can participate in difficult conversations, using silences as a way to observe ego rather than fearing its assessments after the conversation.

Gasshō

ch

Saying What Is So

It's rare for two people to communicate from a "we" perspective. Even when we do begin our communication on the same page, those oppositional voices in the head can quickly move us into adversarial positions.

Of course, I can work on whatever is going on with me on my own. But I'm in a relationship with another person. Why not include that other person? Bottom line is that I want to get clear about any unexamined beliefs, assumptions, and expectations I'm holding. For example, will I be okay if my partner says no? Am I prepared to continue using my communication exploration skills to look deeper? Am I clear that this Awareness Practice I'm doing is first and foremost for me?

From that clarity, we may choose to communicate what's going on with us. "I'm really nervous that you're going to get upset." "I'm not sure what I want to say about this." "I feel confused about what's true and what isn't." What we're doing is revealing our own internal process, not telling someone what they're doing wrong or how their way of being is not working for us or how they need to change. Saying what is so is NOT "speaking my truth." "Speaking my truth" is often code for giving voice to ego/conditioning. Saying what is so is being present to our experience and being willing to communicate from it.

How this is received is not the point. If what we say is not well received, we can remind ourselves that it only takes one person at a time choosing Unconditional Love to transform a relationship. We can choose that Unconditional Love for ourselves and let it expand out from there.

Dear Cheri,
    When communicating with my partner, if I can start from a "yes, and..." place, rather than defensiveness we end with clear communication. Remembering this in

the moment is the difficult thing. My habitual
response usually is defensiveness.
Sincerely,
Defensive

Dear Defensive,
     It sounds as if there might be an opening
for some support in this? Maybe put up a note
for yourself as a reminder. Should you be
feeling really gutsy, if you forget, ask your
partner to help you remember the "yes, and."

Breaking the habit of letting ego
convince us that our loved ones
are out to get us is way up toward the top
of the "Relationship Strengthening"
to-do list—or should be!

     You could say to your partner: "I have a
conditioned habit to be defensive. I don't want
to be defensive with you. I love you. Help me
remember to show that love when we talk,
please."
Gasshō,
ch

Dear Cheri,
    I was working with the
recorder as you suggested and I
found myself stunned by
something that I recorded. I realized that I
wanted to be seen for what I am and
appreciated. Where communication fails in my
relationship is when that need is not being met.
Should I tell my partner that what I need her
to do is to show me more appreciation?
Sincerely,
Needing Appreciation

Dear Needing Appreciation,
    Well, maybe. We're trained to believe
that our loved ones should read our minds. If
they loved us, they would know what we want
and give it to us without our needing to ask. If I
have to tell my partner what I want, even if
s/he then gives it to me, that somehow doesn't
count. That often get turns into "but you only
did it because I asked you to," again feeding the
belief that real love *includes* mind-reading.
    Communicating what we want is a great
option, and there's an even better one. We're

meant to believe (not an accident as the voices harp on it constantly) that everything we want has to come from someone else, that perfect person "out there" who will swoop in and save us from all unhappiness. (You've heard that somewhere perhaps?)

> It can seem to take forever
> to see that the "someone"
> we want to see and hear us, is us.

No, no, no, no, no, screams ego. I don't want me. I want someone else. That is emphatically as true for us as it is for ego! Nobody wants to be seen or heard by ego, not even ego! What we want to be seen and heard by is Authenticity. Center. The Intelligence That Animates. The Divine. What we truly Are. That's what we want to be seen, heard, loved, embraced, accepted, and appreciated by.

It's simple and easy to have that relationship with Authentic Nature when we learn to communicate with the Mentor through Recording and Listening practice.

With all that clear, back to the partner. It can be fun and loving in a relationship to assist one another to be successful. "Hints" usually don't land. We miss them. We all do. We see through our own filters, our own lenses. It's kind to help one another out. If I just spent the whole day cleaning out that nightmare junk depository we euphemistically call the pantry, I'm not going to wait for you to notice. If you had noticed you might already have cleaned it out! So, I do the "let's be successful together" thing (rather than ego's "let's make a contest you will lose" thing). I take you by the hand, lead you to the pantry, explain what I did and give you your lines. I let you know it is now the right time for you to say something like, "Oh, wow, that is *incredible*. That's beautiful! I can't believe you did that. Thank you!" Once the two of you get the hang of this, "failure to appreciate" will be a thing of the past in your even-more-intimate intimate relationship. Gasshō, ch

Dear Cheri,

My communication difficulties arise around my children. We have a rule about bedtime and my kids are always challenging those boundaries. There is always something that gets forgotten that has to be done before going to bed. They don't sit down to dinner on time or it takes too long to do homework. They forget their homework. I've pleaded, cajoled, threatened and yelled. If I let the rule slide, I feel bad. If I yell at them I feel bad. There must be a way to communicate I mean what I say when I say bedtime is at 9:15 p.m.

Sincerely,
Sincere Parent

Dear Sincere Parent,

Ego is a master at "mooshing." It manages to moosh things together, making it appear as if thoughts and behaviors that have nothing to do with one another are related. Enforcing your children's bedtime gets confused with not being a good and loving parent. If you say to your kids...

-- You didn't finish dinner on time, but you're going to bed now and you're likely to be hungry before breakfast.
-- You didn't finish your homework, so you'll probably hear from your teacher.
-- You're still in your clothes at bedtime, so you sleep in your clothes.

...you will likely hear ego voices scream: "Cruel! Heartless! You'll scar those children for life! What kind of parent are you?" But if you also added: "I love you kids like crazy! Now get in bed," there is both clarity and kindness. No one is confused by the love or the requirement.

When we say what we mean and mean what we say, when we're clear and committed, we can trust ourselves. Until we trust ourselves we cannot trust anyone else. Clarity is kindness and with practice we're learning to be clear with kindness. This is not about being a

good person or a bad person. THAT'S the
fuzziness ego oozes into the situation.

Will this be easy with children or with
ourselves? Not if we've lived in fuzziness. We
have to take responsibility. We have to stop
believing the meanings the voices of ego put on
everything.
Gasshō,
ch

Dear Cheri,
I feel extreme discomfort in
communicating to my partner
about something I project we feel
differently about. I want her to go home and
she wants to stay. I believe that I must assert
myself or I won't get my needs met. There is a
long history of these conversations not going
well when I do that. I really want to be in a
relationship in which I am allowed to articulate
what I want without creating distance.
Sincerely,
Just wanting a night alone

Dear Just wanting a night alone,

Nothing like leaping in and practicing to build trust, eh? What might happen if you said something along the lines of, "I love you more than anything and I don't want you to think I don't, and I'd really like to have some time to just focus on me tonight"?

We need reassurance that we're loved because we're deeply conditioned to believe "If you loved me, you would...." Perhaps, in this case, "If you loved me, you would want me to stay, you would want to spend time with me instead of be alone."

Those voices have a tendency to confuse love and action when those have nothing to do with each other. And perhaps your love for her can be expressed by staying with her listening and reflecting, long enough for her to work through some of her reactions. In this way you get to model the way you want the relationship to be.

Gasshō,

ch

Dear Cheri,

Communication with my partner becomes an opportunity to lash out rather than share. A few months ago, I realized how challenging I can be to communicate with! I become a completely different person when we're attempting to communicate. I usually feel attacked and go on the defensive rather than saying what I mean. We just go in circles around this attack/defended process. It feels hopeless.
Sincerely,
Feeling hopeless

Dear Feeling hopeless,

It's not as hopeless as the voices want you to believe it is. Your insight about not being as easy to communicate with as you'd thought (I would say, as you'd been *told* by the voices in conditioned mind) is huge and powerful. That's exactly the kind of thing ego works to make sure we *never* see. Congratulations.

But consider this. Do you assume your partner doesn't know when you become "someone" else? People close to us can usually tell when we're "not ourselves;" they just tend not to tell us, as feedback like that is often not well received by egocentric karmic conditioning/self-hate.

Let me ask you this: What stops you from saying to her what you just said to me? We are conditioned to believe that communication has to be about solving the issue at hand so it never happens again. Isn't it more intimate to start by saying what happens to you when you attempt to communicate? To share your process? That's a potentially irresistible invitation to authentic communication.
Gasshō,
ch

Dear Cheri,
Whenever I want to communicate appreciation, gratitude, or love it becomes a BIG DEAL. It feels like life and death to get the words just right for my message to be well-received and not misunderstood.

I get paralyzed, second-guess, question how sincere I sound, wonder whether I am over the top, etc. And most of the time I don't end up expressing what I want to say. People end up thinking that I am unloving and unappreciative.
Sincerely,
Struggling to express nice things

Dear Struggling to express nice things,
     It does feel like life and death, but it's ego's death, not yours.
     If you went right ahead and said what you love, what you're grateful for, what you appreciate, ego would cease to exist. Expressing from Authenticity implies we're no longer attending to ego, and ego lives on our attention.

267

The voices will do anything to stop you from saying something loving, kind, or appreciative.

So, you see what you must do, yes? When something drops in to say, you have to say it. That's it. No way to soften the blow! However, this is not a contest so how about you start by doing that once a day?

Gasshō,

ch

Dear Cheri,

I find myself in a state of complete anxiety when I'm put on the spot and asked a question. I usually blurt something out or just mumble something and feel like a complete fool afterwards. Do you have any suggestions for me?

Sincerely,

Anxious Communicator

Dear Anxious Communicator,

Most of us learned early on that "you need to say something NOW and you need to say it perfectly." We get one shot and if we don't score a direct hit, we've failed.

It's not okay to ask for some time to reflect.
It's not okay to go back and clarify.
It's not okay to acknowledge what we said was not as clear or accurate as we would wish.

But, of course, it's okay. It's only not okay for the judgmental voice in the head setting us up for a beating later.

What if, when we find ourselves in one of those "on the spot, need to say something NOW" situations, we practice stopping, taking a long deep breath, and saying something along these lines: "I get so nervous when I try to think on my feet that I find myself becoming quite inarticulate. Please ask whatever clarifying questions might help us both, and please be patient as I stumble along."

Now, are there people in the world who would take advantage of that level of sincerity? Of course. And we can feel sorry for them. They're in the grip of self-hate, and, thus, their opinion need not concern us. We can be polite and hope that as they wake up out of the self-hate that is causing them to behave that way, they will awaken gradually enough that they'll choose compassion for themselves rather than self-hate.

Gasshō,

ch

Dear Cheri

I am absolutely dumbstruck when someone makes a racist comment at a dinner party. Someone always does it, and I'm at a loss in terms of how to respond. I want to lash out. I want to point out how inappropriate such a remark is, but I can't find the words or the willingness to do it. I guess I'm afraid to speak out, afraid to rock the boat, afraid to make a scene. And afterwards, I feel bad because I could not stand up for what I believe in.

Sincerely,

At a loss

Dear At a loss,

Have you ever considered the possibility that what you're really afraid of is what the voices say will be the consequences of speaking out? In other words, you're believing what that conversation in your head says will happen when you say something. Until you say something, you'll never know what will actually happen.

Fortunately, as a practitioner of awareness you can start small. You can be with your experience of what happens for you when someone makes a racist joke. For instance, you could simply say it hurts your heart when you hear something like that.

Gasshō,

ch

Dear Cheri,

I don't feel heard. When that happens, I go to a childish place of "Why bother saying anything. No one cares what you have to say anyway." I just stop talking and retreat.

Sincerely,

Feeling Unheard

Dear Feeling Unheard,

You're in a situation in which it appears to you that the person you're talking with is not listening to you. The ego voices give you an interpretation of the situation. "They aren't listening. They don't care. What you're saying doesn't matter anyway," which triggers a conditioned reaction: "Don't say anything."

If you don't believe that conversation in your head, it's perfectly possible to say, "I sense you're not hearing me. Is this not a good time to talk?" This might assist the other person to come to and really listen to you. It might help them look at whether or not they can listen to you, and they might respond honestly as to whether or not it's a good time to talk. If they get offended or upset, then you know it's not a good time to say anything to them, not because what you have to say is not important, but because they're too busy listening to a conversation in *their* head to be attending to you.

Gasshō

ch

Dear Cheri,

My husband left on a business trip for two weeks. During that time, he barely spoke to me and the children. I felt divorced, like I had no husband or we had separated. I projected he was angry about something. When I confronted him on his return, he apologized for being unavailable but gave me no indication why he didn't call or talk to me. How can I get him to communicate about what's going on with him?

Sincerely,

Forlorn

Dear Forlorn,

Have you asked him whether he was angry? That's something obvious that rarely occurs to us to do.

But I bet even though you didn't ask him about his experience, there were many reasons ego concocted in your head to explain his behavior. Perhaps there were speculations, angry rants, tales casting you as a victim, etc. Those voices are happy to talk to you, but will do everything to keep you from having an actual conversation with him.

This might be a great opportunity for a discussion. You could let your husband know that voices in your head (if that's a familiar concept to him and he won't assume you became mentally ill while he was gone) were telling you his lack of communication meant he was angry. You could ask him, "Were you angry?" Be interesting to hear his side, huh? You could tell him that you felt "divorced" while he was gone and wasn't communicating.

BACK & FORTH

You could tell him how you feel, and then ask about his experience. *Really listen* as he talks with you. Back and forth, sharing perspectives, hearing one another, gaining clarity.

Now, there's the possibility that initially he won't be forthcoming. That's okay. You're letting him know what's going on with you. You're owning your projections. You're talking about *your experience*, not about him. If he has nothing to say, you can just thank him for listening. Here's a really important piece:

Whatever you receive from him, you can process with the Mentor using your recorder.
Gasshō,
ch

Dear Cheri,
    What do I do when I'm the victim of unkind communication from my partner? I can stay present and listen, but what is said hurts my feelings. I just can't believe she would know me and say something like that about me. I know I don't need to take it personally, but I do. Do I need to protect myself from the unkind words of another person?
Sincerely,
Hurt Feelings

Dear Hurt Feelings,
    Nope. We don't need to protect ourselves from other people. What we do need protection from is egocentric karmic conditioning/self-hate! Let's go to the other side of this.

You say something to your partner. She gets her feelings hurt. Did you mean for what you said to hurt her feelings? No. Might you have said what you said from a place of hurt feelings? Might it have been one of those, "You upset me and I'm going to get back at you" times? Sure. We all know those places. But here's where we want to get with this: You're partners. You love one another, care about one another, aren't just sticking together to save on the rent. Rather than waste precious moments "hurting one another" because you've "hurt one another" (which is nonsense, by the way, as "hurt feelings" are ALWAYS a story put forth by ego to justify ego's actions), you can communicate. "Wow, that landed like a blow. I'm sure you didn't mean to hurt me. Can we talk about what's going on here?" You're practicing getting to and staying in conscious compassionate awareness.

If she (or anyone) said to you, "You are an awful person and I hate you," would you really want to take that seriously, personally, and get involved with it? Would you want to leave center, wellbeing, lovingkindness, joy, and

peace for *that?* For *anything?* Of course not.
And especially not for ego's "hurt feelings."
Gasshō,
ch

Dear Cheri,
    I'm afraid to be vulnerable in
communication, which is why I don't say what's
going on for me.
Sincerely,
Not saying what is so

Dear Not saying what is so,
    We're all conditioned to believe we're
"safe" if the only thing we're in communication
with is those voices in our head. The moment
we consider being vulnerable, those voices
ramp up and we retreat, believing the situation
or the person we're interacting with is the
problem. That way, we don't get to see that *it's
the ego conversation* that is causing us to
retreat, not the situation or the other person.

Which is what I love about communication. We actually get to speak back and forth with someone until we get to clarity. No more "I hear something in my head about you," "you hear something in your head about me," and "neither of us can say anything because we're convinced what we're hearing in the head is true."

Outside of the ego conversation, there are no mistakes and no hurt feelings. All can be said and received because there's no ego to get hurt or offended. What does this take? *Practice.* We're not going for success, getting it right, avoiding making a mistake, or any other ego nonsense. We're practicing awareness, and communication is our vehicle.

Gasshō,

ch

Dear Cheri,

    I watch my partner do things that are not good for him. He's not in good health but he won't take care of himself. He won't do the things that would help him. If I say something, he gets angry and upset with me. If I don't say something, I feel resentful. It's awful of me to say but part of why I want him to take care of himself comes from my fear of losing him. If he cared about me at all, he might consider taking care of himself?

Sincerely,
Frustrated

Dear Frustrated,

Attempting to communicate with a loved one about something they don't want to talk about is challenging. You're concerned. It seems to you your loved one is in danger. But you're afraid to say anything. What if you offend? What if what you say is met with anger? Rejection? What if this puts a permanent rent in your relationship?

You know that not saying anything is causing problems in the relationship. The choice is to say nothing and let those problems grow or risk saying something that might put the two of you on a path to more open communication.

What we can be fairly sure about is that NOT attempting a communication WILL eventually put a permanent rent in the relationship. You'll watch the situation, continuing to see it as dangerous, with a growing resentment that you're not allowed to do something to care for someone you care about.

How about this as an alternative: Start with a conversation about your trepidation about saying anything. "I want to talk with you about something that's concerning me about you and I'm afraid to do it. My fear is that you'll feel I'm trying to control you or am interfering or some such thing, and it will cause problems in our relationship." See what he says.

We must be clear that even the best communication won't solve all our worldly issues. He might continue to choose behaviors that are harmful to him. The result of this might be that you lose him sooner than you want, yes, but more important, sooner than you believe you need to. You may not have a choice in any of that. It's always our work to get to a place of well-being regardless of circumstances. You can communicate what you want him to know and his life is still up to him. Your practice is what will resolve your resentment and fear of loss, letting you make peace with your lack of control in the situation.

Gasshō,

ch

Dear Cheri,
 I experimented with asking for what I wanted. I host a weekly meeting and I provide the refreshments. I made a request that everyone attending the meeting contribute something. This was hard for me to do, but I did it. And it was disastrous. Some of the regulars didn't show up for the meeting. Those who came without food felt they could not eat. And I felt bad!

Sincerely,
A host without attendees

Dear A host without attendees,

We're looking at communication, right? We're not benefitted in that exploration by *listening* to what the voices of egocentric karmic conditioning/self-hate tell us and then *concluding* what we should do because of that. Tying "how it goes" to "acceptance" is an ego bamboozle par excellence. How about

communicating? How about asking people to help you solve the issue? Maybe there doesn't need to be food. Maybe those who want to eat can bring a "sack lunch." Maybe people could take turns providing a meal. Maybe....So many alternatives if we aren't listening to that limiting conversation in conditioned mind.

Remember: Communicating once doesn't necessarily mean that more communicating won't be required.

Gasshō,

ch

Cede Your Position

One of ego's favorite ploys is to convince us that "I need to take a stand for me." I need to assert my opinion, defend my point of view, and persuade you that I'm right.

Since the "I" here is ego,
the only stand we would be taking
would be for it.

What's sacrificed is connection with another person. In communication, we learn that winning can be the result of ceding, rather than holding, our position. Because what we cede is ego's position. And we're fine with that.

Dear Cheri,
I'm not always present when I communicate with my partner. I'm

often unskillful in what I say to her. I've followed your guidance to say to her that it was "not me" saying what I said. I was simply being a spokesperson for the voices of ego. Sometimes she says she understands. On occasion, she has asked me not to use identification with ego as an excuse and to take responsibility for my actions. I'm not sure what to do with that. If I go unconscious and let the voices speak through me, how am I responsible for that?

Sincerely,
Wanting to take responsibility

Dear Wanting to take responsibility,

Lots of folks, receiving this kind of admittedly true and right-on-target "helpful information" from a partner, would allow ego to leap in and go after her. "How dare she be so judgmental and critical of you, implying you make excuses and don't take responsibility, when you're trying so hard." That would, of course, lead to a breakdown in what you're attempting to achieve through communication.

You didn't fall for that! Congratulations.

It's not my experience that we should take responsibility for what we do when identified with egocentric karmic conditioning/self-hate. (Trying to do that is a good definition of self-hate.) What we *can* and *should* take responsibility for is ending identification with egocentric karmic conditioning/self-hate. That's what practicing awareness is all about.

For example: I forget to pick up something on the way home from work, am asked about it when I come in, and fly into a rage. "I have so much on my mind, how the deuce am I supposed to remember to pick up stuff!" This is delivered at the top of my lungs, accompanied by a lot of stomping and throwing things around. The fact is I forgot to pick it up. I was distracted, noodling around in conditioned mind, talking on the phone...whatever.

Taking responsibility is saying, "Drat. I forgot. Can I go get it now, or can it wait until tomorrow?"

When you've said something unskillful, you can say, "Apologies, I was unskillful. What I meant to say is...." That's taking responsibility rather than blaming ego.

Be patient.
We've been lost in conditioned mind
for a long time, and waking up
is bound to take longer than we wish it would.
Be grateful and happy that working
to awaken is what you choose to do.

Gasshō,
ch

Dear Cheri,
    When my partner gets angry,
he tends to lash out at me. Instead
of saying something in response, I retreat and
play the event over and over in my head. He is
always "wrong" and could have done it
differently. I am left feeling shame and hurt.
Don't know what to say. Start feeling angry
back. Cycle continues. Much is left unsaid and
resentment builds.
Sincerely,
Resentful

Dear Resentful,

Does he know any of this? Have you told him what your process is and what this does to you and, therefore, to the relationship? If he's open to it, you could ask if he'd be willing to practice communicating with you in a way that would assist you to get out of this hurtful, harmful cycle. I remember reading years ago about a couples therapist who taught her clients to say to one another, "I'm sure you have a very good reason for what you said/did, would you please tell me what that is?" Then the facilitation tools of Reflecting, Drawing Out, and Clarifying come into play. Obviously, it would be easiest if both partners were willing to engage, but that's not technically a requirement. One person, devoted to saving a relationship and making it intimate, loving, and strong can do the work for two. On the other hand, maintaining a position of resentful, injured party only supports ego.

All of these behavior changes are best practiced in the calm times. Perhaps you propose going out for a walk for the express purpose of talking about a difficult topic. Be

sure you talk about **you**. How you feel, what happens with you, that you don't want anything to come between the two of you, that you don't want to withdraw and feel resentful. Remember, you're the one who wants to initiate the conversation. Give him some time to get used to this new way of being together. And, again, your job is to express what is so for you and hear whatever he may choose to say. Then you process what happens with the Mentor. You want to make this as safe as possible for the two of you as your back and forth communication picks up speed.
Gasshō,
ch

Dear Cheri,
    I'm not good at holding back. I blurt something out, it's often unskillful, and I always feel bad afterwards. How do I stay present enough not to just react?
Sincerely,
Reactive

Dear Reactive,

Blessedly, when we blurt stuff out we can always "take a mulligan."

I'M TAKING A MULLIGAN!

Just say, "Oops, that is not what I meant; let me try again." Folks are often grateful they don't have to get hostile with us. We can even let people know when we're working on a project like this. "I've realized that I...." Let them in on the *process* and most folks will be supportive and understanding. If not, that's okay. You're the one practicing awareness!
Gasshō,
ch

Dear Cheri,

My partner and I get into fights about this process. He wants input on a project. I offer him my suggestions. He

289

listens to everything I have to say and then simply does what he wants to do. Most often that does not involve doing anything I suggest! It's frustrating. I want to scream and say, "Why did you ask me in the first place if you don't really want my input?" But I don't. I just stay silent and fume and vow to myself that if I am asked again, I won't respond. But I always do and we end up in this place where an attempt to communicate and connect leads to disconnect and anger.

Sincerely,

Frustrated

Dear Frustrated,

I used to have an unconscious habit that made folks around me gnash their teeth. We're going out to eat and I'm asked where I'd like to go. "I don't know. What do you think?" Other person would start listing possibilities. Italian? Chinese? Japanese? Ethiopian? French? Russian? American? On go the choices as I stare off into the far distance. Finally the possibilities are exhausted and I say, "Italian sounds good." The burning question for the other person is, "Why did you make me go through all that if what you wanted was Italian? That was the first option mentioned!" But I didn't *know* I wanted Italian until I had the chance to "taste" all the other possibilities in my mind. Perhaps your partner has a process along those lines. Perhaps he wants to hear everyone's ideas as a way of "tasting" his options so he can get clear about what he wants to do. You might be indispensable in his process. Perhaps you *are* "helping" him, just not in a way conditioning recognizes. How about asking him? Calmly, after the anger has passed.

Gasshō,

ch

Dear Cheri,

I want my partner to be there for me when I'm anxious and worried, but he refuses. It hurts my feelings. I'm there for him when he needs me, but when I need him he's MIA.

Sincerely,

Hurt

Dear Hurt,

Here we have the familiar "one side of the story." In my world, I'm doing everything right. I'm meeting all—well, most—of my standards for being a good, supportive partner. Why can't he do the same? The simple answer is that my standards are not his standards. So, what are his standards? We don't know. Fortunately, we have all the resources needed to find out.

ASK?!

My hurt feelings (always a dead giveaway that ego has slipped into the driver's seat) want me to FIND OUT! Grill him. Pin him to the wall. (There is anger behind those hurt feelings, right?) But that's not what we want to do. This is my partner. This is someone I love, someone I want to understand. So, we begin a gentle, two-pronged inquiry. There's no hurry. The first prong is your worry and anxiety issue. That's really not his to resolve; it's yours. The second prong is an exploration of what goes on with him when you're feeling anxious and worried.

Perhaps it makes him anxious and worried! We don't know but it will be interesting to find out.

Ego would have us believe that our problems are the result of how other people are.
They aren't.
Our problems are, without exception, the result of our relationship with ego.

So, as you work to move through your relationship with anxiety and worry, and as you gently explore with your partner what goes on with him when he seems unavailable to you, you're going to benefit enormously. And, we hope he feels he's benefiting enormously as well.
Gasshō,
ch

Do It as a Practice

Awareness Practice is one, big, lifelong experiment. Mahatma Gandhi spoke about his "experiments in truth," which is what we're practicing. What's true? What's real? How do we know? How can we find out?  If we want clarity we have to risk confronting that harsh voice in the head that has a long history of silencing us.

We must keep in mind that we are *practicing* awareness and presence. If you took up a musical instrument or a foreign language you wouldn't expect yourself to be proficient the first time out. (Though the voices of self-hate will begin to add their critical judgments in a ridiculously short time.)

In Awareness Practice, we go into a challenging situation *for the purpose of* attempting to stay conscious and present. We start conscious. Before long, we're caught by egocentric karmic conditioning/self-hate and we're gone. When we come to, we pick up the recorder and record our insights. The negative voices don't get to speak. We're gaining clarity. "Ah, I see. I got distracted there and forgot which note comes next." Distracted. Got it. Now I'm aware of distraction as I begin my next experiment.

Dear Cheri,
	Speaking in front of a group intimidates me. I may have a story to tell, but if I try my voice and body tremble and I feel ashamed and inept.
Sincerely,
Ashamed and Inept

Dear Ashamed and Inept,
	When I was first sent out by my teacher to do workshops on meditation, I would stammer, turn a hideous shade of red, and shake so badly I could hardly sit on my

meditation cushion. In the ensuing years, I've spoken with thousands and thousands of people in every possible venue—without a stammer, a blush, or a shake. What happened to create that change? PRACTICE. I just did it over and over and over until it became completely comfortable. We've all had that experience countless times. We walk, we speak, we drive, we cook, we type...If the voices of self-hate had been in place when we were a year old, the way they are in adulthood, we would never have learned to walk, speak, or use the bathroom! What can now take you through the process from tremble/shame/inept to nothing wrong/having fun/enjoying life? Approaching the whole thing as a workshop *that's for your benefit* and supported by R/L and the Mentor. Gasshō,
ch

Dear Cheri,
    Someone asked if she could have my shelves and I'd use hers. I like mine better. I said no, but felt bad about

it. Ugh! So, my communication challenge is that I normally say yes to what someone wants but I don't really want to. What should I do? Say yes, anyway?
Sincerely,
Puzzled

Dear Puzzled,
That "Ugh!" is the payoff for ego's controlling machinations. Whatever we do we're meant to wind up in Ugh, feeling bad. You say no you feel bad; you say yes you feel bad. We lose, ego wins. So, here's a way to practice with it.

For a week, each time someone asks you for something you say, "Gosh, I'd love to, but I'm going to have to say no." You can look sincerely disappointed if you choose.  You're not lying. You're in a workshop, and the exercise in the workshop is to say that.

For another week, each time someone asks you for something you say, "Yes, I can do that." You look excited. Now the exercise in the workshop is to say yes. What this simple, challenging exercise does is to break the deeply conditioned, knee jerk connection between "something happens" and "look to conditioned mind for what to do." Because you already know what you're going to say, you don't need to hesitate for those few beats that allow ego to slip in and take over. You're in a workshop. This automatically positions you to be looking at the whole, at the larger process, rather than following ego's tunnel vision to "what should I do?" Now you're in a position to see all sorts of things you've been prevented from being aware of—such as you don't have only one option in a situation.

Watch really closely what happens in each circumstance and talk it over with the Mentor via R/L.
Gasshō,
ch

Dear Cheri,
I had a call with my sister recently. She was upset. She wanted to know why I hadn't called earlier to share the

"bad news." "Bad news doesn't get better with age," I heard her say. I felt bad but I had done my best. Perhaps I should have called earlier!
Sincerely,
Should have Known

Dear Should have Known
     I project you're seeing that nothing valuable comes from ego's reviews. **We see what we see and get what we get when we see it and get it.** Egocentric karmic conditioning/ self-hate has mountains of "adages" that support its perspective. People believe profoundly that it's possible to make a mistake and it's possible to have "known better" and that if they'd done something different back then they'd have the life they want now. There are people who clearly, as you've noted, believe there really are such things as good news and bad news, there is a better and a worse, and time is what makes all the difference. It's all nonsense. The fact that most people believe something doesn't make that something true. The net result of the whole process is suffering.

All that matters about anything is how we are with it.

Did you see something? Learn something? Are you choosing to realize you're doing your best, to let yourself relax and breathe rather than going with a beating from self-hate? That seems like a lot to get. It's hard to see all that learning and growth as a mistake, isn't it?

It might be helpful to see every call with your sister as a workshop in awareness and communication. Decide what you want to practice on the call. Get clear about that with the Mentor before the call. Once the call is done, record what you see. Then let the Mentor help you choose what you want to practice on the next call. In this way, calls with your sister can move from suffering to fun.

Gasshō,

ch

Dear Cheri,

I don't say what I want to say because I don't believe I'll be understood. It's dangerous to let people know I exist, take up space, or have an opinion. I can't show I'm needy. And when I attempt to speak, the sensations in my body are so intense that it feels like I won't survive!

Sincerely,

Won't survive sensations

Dear Won't survive sensations,

The sensations you experience as you listen to and believe the voices are meant to convince you that *your* survival is at stake. It's not! It's ego's survival those voices are protecting. If you speak up, the identity being maintained through believing the threats will not survive. That identity is ego, not you. As you get clearer about those threats, you'll realize that taking your rightful place in Life is an option not survivable **for ego.**

So, let's start small, huh? Find a time and place that feels safe for you to step out a bit. *Consciously* choose to add something to the conversation. Watch everything that happens as you do. When you're alone, record what you saw. Listen. Any insights from that? Record those insights. Find another time and place. You get the idea, right? Remember, small. Don't let those same voices turn this into a competition that you're bound to lose. You're learning to hear what the voices say and learning not to believe them.

Gasshō,

ch

Dear Cheri,

   In charged political situations, the reflexive reaction is to attempt to be reasonable, and let someone else take the lead. There's fear of confrontation. Intellectually I see that it doesn't have to be that way, but I have resistance to putting myself out there. I wish I could be peaceful in the face of anger. But I retreat because I can't get myself to go beyond my fear.

Sincerely,

Fearful

Dear Fearful,

This sounds like another one of those perfect "start small" situations. Those voices always want us to see a conditioned reaction and either be finished with it all at once or believe we're a hopeless failure and need to give up. You've already seen how charged situations produce retreat and withdrawal behaviors. Now, you can practice taking small steps not to fall for that ego identification.

Remember, you can always drop back and regroup for the next opportunity. You're a scientist. You're doing experiments. "What happens when this...?" "What happens when I...?" As soon as you realize you're in one of "those" situations, move into a "bring peace amidst anger" orientation.
-- Bring attention to your breath.
-- Feel your feet on the floor.
-- Notice each of your senses.

Stay with that for as long as you can remain conscious, and when conditioning roars in—as it will—just smile and nod. At first you may add only one sentence to the conversation. It doesn't matter. It doesn't matter what you

say or don't say, how long you can stay present,
or how quickly you go unconscious.

Your only assignment is to see
what egocentric karmic conditioning/self-hate
has been doing to you,
and, small step by small step,
put it out of business.

Gasshō,
ch

OUT OF BUSINESS

In Gasshō

"The deepest level of communication is not communication, but communion. It is wordless ... beyond speech ... beyond concept."
— Thomas Merton

"Out beyond ideas of wrongdoing
and rightdoing there is a field.
I'll meet you there.
When the soul lies down in that grass
the world is too full to talk about."
— Rumi

"Words!
The Way is beyond language,
for in it there is
no yesterday
no tomorrow
no today."
— Seng T'san

Spiritual sages of all times and traditions tell us about communion, the blissful state of non-separation that exists when the ego doesn't. Communion is union, connectedness, harmony, a continuity of oneness.

Human beings have the unique ability to experience themselves as separate. At the interface of something "other," this continuity of oneness is interrupted by a registration of "difference." Differences, it appears, are parsed by an orientation of separation into a "me" other than "you," instead of a "me and you." Imagine how different the world might be if differences were interesting and encounters a chance to extend our awareness of the multiplicity of the world rather than an occasion to defend boundaries. In spiritual practice we unlearn a perspective, which reorients our perception, replacing the lens of separation with awareness of the oneness of all things.

Compassion is often defined as being able to "be with," a "complete" or "wholehearted" acceptance of how things are. Compassionate communication can assist us to bridge "differences" and achieve the clarity that returns us to connectedness. But conditioning gets in the way.

In the form of a ceaseless conversation in the head, ego, the illusion of a self that is separate from Life, scrambles communication. Identified with ego, we will not say what we want to say, and we will say what we should not say, and differences rather than harmony are the result when we "communicate." That maintains ego, but it does nothing for the human being!

We practice authentic communication when we bypass ego identification and come to presence, present to how ego is maintaining separation. From that vantage point of awareness, we choose not to be the voice of ego. We reveal our process, what ego may be saying or doing to us, as a way to establish a communication bridge that cannot be intercepted by ego. We Reflect, Draw Out, and Clarify as techniques to keep ego out of an interaction with another human being. And when ego does hijack the communication, which it surely will, we pick up the recorder and reestablish our connection to the wisdom, love, and compassion that we Are. From compassion, we attempt once more to communicate, and that communication has the possibility of getting us to communion.

"Gasshō," the salutation at the end of each of the letters, is a Japanese word that accompanies the gesture of bringing hands together at the heart and bowing. It's a sacred ritual gesture, sometimes defined as "my heart and your heart are one." It embodies the possibility available to all of us of a return to the state of Oneness, where all opposites are reconciled. Gasshō is the attitude of mind that we can adopt in our attempts to communicate.

Communication then becomes a spiritual practice, embodying reverence, respect, and compassion in words as we move in The Way towards the wordless.

Dear Cheri,
    I initiated a conversation about a taboo topic with my husband. I asked him to describe his process, and really listened, reflecting him closely. Turns out I had been wrongly taking his actions personally. That felt like such a success!
Sincerely,
Feeling Successful

Dear Feeling Successful,
    WELL DONE! Out of the closet and into the Present! Do you know that old joke about being a mushroom? I'm a mushroom because, like mushrooms, I'm kept in the dark and fed, manure (attempting to avoid profanity in a practice setting, you see). We are ego's mushrooms. You weren't allowed to talk about certain topics with your partner because he would get upset and reject you. It was better

to feel fear and isolation than to risk the loss of love that would result if you dared bring up an upsetting subject with him. Turns out that was a pack of lies, a giant load of mushroom food. You *practiced*. You talked with the Mentor, you turned to your awareness practice for guidance, and *you communicated with him!* He didn't throw you across the room or refuse to engage with you—**he talked with you.** He talked and you listened and reflected. The whole ego-fear-fueled drama collapsed. That wasn't what you were being told inside conditioned mind! The voices were lying to you, and you, courageous practitioner of awareness, faced down egocentric karmic conditioning/self-hate and received your reward—freedom, joy, and love.
Gasshō,
ch

Dear Cheri,
    I have been practicing no-ego in communication. In dropping the conversation about my sister's lack of participation, I notice a conversation about being annoyed by her

opinions. It's fun to see ego in operation and not act from it.

Sincerely,
Having Fun

Dear Having Fun,

It is fun! You're seeing that NOTHING that's been about "her" has been about "her," right? Your relationship (we're all right here with you) has never been *with* her. Your relationship has been with a conversation in conditioned mind *about* her. Now you're getting to have a relationship with a real human being, and you're *getting to see the process* egocentric karmic conditioning/self-hate uses to sabotage you, your sister, the relationship, and, most important of all, *being present.* Conversations in the head maintain separation and keep you out of the present for a while. You started looking closer at that, she started participating, and the conversation turned to "she has the most annoying opinions." Separate. Not present. You're onto that! Oh, this IS fun!

Gasshō,
ch

Dear Cheri,
I had a conversation with someone I have difficulty communicating with. I usually avoid talking to them, but for some reason we started up a conversation. It was so odd. I realized that I did not know this person at all! It was a lovely conversation and I experienced such kindness.
Sincerely,
Amazed

Dear Amazed,
Watching how egocentric karmic conditioning/self-hate frames everything (that conversation in conditioned mind we're meant never to see but are always looking through) allows us to enter an entirely new world, doesn't it? Ego would scoff that "whole new world" is a bit grandiose, but it's accurate. I'm looking through eons of egocentric karmic conditioning/self-hate that has landed in this person I call me, and I'm being told by that system that when I look at you, I'm seeing you. How can we believe such a thing? Well, actually, it's easy—we've been brainwashed. We've been

convinced that we are able to look through our unexamined filters and see someone else clearly. Clearly? We can't even see them! Now we're looking in the right direction! And looking in that direction, we get to know someone as they are and experience ourselves as we are.
Gasshō,
ch

Dear Cheri,
        I've been practicing always choosing to communicate, and then sticking around for what happens. No feeling bad, no holding out hope for the worst not to happen. Only confirmation that conditioning lies and is working against me.
Gasshō,
Practicing

Dear Practicing,
        That's it! That's exactly what we're not "supposed" to do, and it is what we must do. In countless situations, egocentric karmic conditioning/self-hate swoops in, does damage,

and races off, leaving a person dazed and bruised. We're then meant to stagger around in a conversation about what we've done wrong until the next swoop. You're not doing that. You see what's happening, you communicate, and you watch what happens next.

Conditioning doesn't have a chance.
It can only operate in the dark.
When you're right there watching,
it has no way to avoid being revealed,
and, once revealed,
it loses its power.

We want to keep at it because we want to be present for every swoop and be there to recognize our freedom each time.
Gasshō,
ch

Dear Cheri,
    I watched this progression...
Something arose to say and I said
it. Right on the heels of that, I heard a voice

say, "Way too direct." I was conscious of feeling self-conscious. The other person didn't seem to notice! I realize that the more I lose interest in how I feel, the less the voices can get me about how others' feel about what I say. I no longer have to second-guess.
Sincerely,
Not Listening to Voices

Dear Not Listening to Voices,
    What can we say to that other than AMEN! That voice in the head distracting, throwing us off through self-consciousness, is then able to "explain" what happened and what we did wrong. Was any of what it said true? NO. It wasn't. As you notice, *by being present to all of it*, the other person didn't skip a beat. The other person wasn't thinking, "Way too direct." That was only happening in *your* head, and *had you not been there*, ego's story would have carried the day. Being in awareness as ego does what it does is where we want to be. Ego "idealizes" our being so "centered" that "ego just never does what it does."

317

NOPE. We want to be here, eyes wide open, paying full attention as it does what it has always done to mess us up. Now we see it. Now we don't fall for it (as often!).
Gasshō,
ch

Work with Cheri Huber

Visit www.cherihuber.com to access Cheri's latest interviews.

Read Cheri's blogs at http://cherispracticeblog.blogspot.com.

To talk with Cheri, call in to Open Air, her internet-based radio show. Archives of the show and instructions on how to participate are available at www.openairwithcherihuber.org

To work with Cheri on an individual basis, sign up for her email classes at schedule.livingcompassion.org.

Visit www.recordingandlistening.org to learn about the practice that is Cheri's passion.

Cheri's books are available from your local independent bookstore or online at www.keepitsimple.org.

Living Compassion

For more information on Zen Awareness Practice and the teachings of Cheri Huber, visit www.livingcompassion.org. Here you can:

- Find a schedule of retreats and workshops
- Locate meditation groups in your area
- Find out more about virtual practice opportunities such as Reflective Listening, Virtual Meditation, Email Classes
- Get information on visiting the Monastery
- Access newsletters and blogs on Zen Awareness Practice
- Sign up for individual or group Zen Awareness Coaching and Recording and Listening Training

Contact

Living Compassion/Zen Monastery Peace Center
P.O. Box 1756
Murphys, CA 95247
Email: information@livingcompassion.org

REGARDLESS OF WHAT YOU WERE TAUGHT TO BELIEVE...

THERE IS NOTHING WRONG WITH YOU

REVISED EDITION

GOING BEYOND SELF-HATE

A COMPASSIONATE PROCESS FOR LEARNING TO
ACCEPT YOURSELF EXACTLY AS YOU ARE

CHERI HUBER

DESIGNED AND ILLUSTRATED BY JUNE SHIVER

There Is Nothing Wrong with You
An Extraordinary Eight-Day Retreat
based on the book
There Is Nothing Wrong with You:
Going Beyond Self-Hate
by Cheri Huber

Inside each of us is a "persistent voice of discontent." It is constantly critical of life, the world, and almost everything we say and do. As children, in order to survive, we learned to listen to this voice and believe what it says.

This retreat is eight days of looking directly at how we are rejected and punished by the voices of self-hate and discovering how to let that go. Through a variety of exercises and periods of group processing, participants gain a clearer perspective on how they live their lives and on how to find compassion for themselves and others.

This work is challenging, joyous, fulfilling, scary, courageous, demanding, freeing, loving, kind, and compassionate — compassionate toward yourself and everyone you will ever know.

For information on attending, contact:
Living Compassion/Zen Monastery Peace Center
P.O. Box 1756
Murphys, CA 95247
Email: information@livingcompassion.org
Website: www.livingcompassion.org

WHAT YOU PRACTICE IS WHAT YOU HAVE

A GUIDE TO
HAVING THE LIFE YOU WANT

CHERI HUBER
AUTHOR OF THERE IS NOTHING WRONG WITH YOU
EDITED AND ILLUSTRATED BY JUNE SHIVER

What You Practice Is What You Have is a follow-up to
There Is Nothing Wrong with You. Here, Cheri further
exposes the lies and antics of self-hate. Included are
Awareness Practice tools, such as Recording and
Listening, for seeing how we are trapped in old patterns
of suffering and for transcending self-hate through
kindness. ISBN 9780971030978

What Universe Are You Creating? is a playful, powerful way to learn the skill of Recording and Listening, a revolutionary tool for practicing turning attention from incessant, haranguing, karmically conditioned patterns of thought and action to the peace of presence. Recording in your own voice and then listening to kind words, encouragement, inspirational readings, favorite songs, gratitude lists, meditations—in short, being your own mentor—turns attention away from the constant stream of negative self-talk, robbing it of its power by revealing its illusory nature. ISBN: 9780991596300

Fear is not what we think it is. It is possible to find within ourselves the experience of life that was ours before we were taught to be afraid. *The Fear Book* shows us how to recognize fear for what it is and how to overcome its devastating effects through a series of awareness practice exercises, including the powerful Recording and Listening tool.
ISBN: 9780991596324

Written in a humorous and lighthearted style, *The Big Bamboozle* illustrates through essays, stories, and examples what keeps us from choosing love, happiness, and joy. The book includes a year of practical exercises and nuggets of wisdom from those who have practiced with these teachings.
ISBN: 9780991596317